Humanities Curriculum Guidelines
for the Middle and Secondary Years

Humanities Curriculum Guidelines
for the Middle and Secondary Years

An Inservice Training Document
prepared by
Keith J Driscoll
In the Northamptonshire Education Department

 The Falmer Press

(A member of the Taylor & Francis Group)
London and Philadelphia

223459

373,19
D 781

| UK | The Falmer Press, Falmer House, Barcombe, Lewes, East Sussex, BN8 5DL |
| USA | The Falmer Press, Taylor & Francis Inc., 242 Cherry Street, Philadelphia, PA 19106-1906 |

First published 1986

Library of Congress Cataloging-in-Publication Data

Driscoll, Keith J.
    Humanities curriculum guidelines for the middle and secondary years.
    Bibliography: P.
    1. Humanities—Study and teaching (Secondary)—England—Northamptonshire. 2. Middle schools—England—Northamptonshire—Curricula. 3. High schools—England—Northamptonshire—Curricula. I. Title.
AZ183.G7D75 1986   373.198'0712   86-9007
ISBN 1-85000-120-0
ISBN 1-85000-121-9 (pbk.)

Typset in 11/12 Caledonia
Imago Publishing Ltd, Thame, Oxon.

Printed in Great Britain by Taylor & Francis (Printers) Ltd, Basingstoke

Contents

It is necessary to stress that this publication is intended for use as a handbook on in-service training courses so that some of the diagrammatic material within it is not necessarily closely related to the text but relates to the components of an in-service training programme.

Foreword

The reasons for the production of this guideline on humanities teaching in the secondary and middle years are the following:

Firstly, I hope that it will act as a discussion document for people concerned with the teaching of humanities subjects in the middle years and, to a large extent, throughout the secondary years.

Secondly, the outline should allow people to contribute from their own areas of special concern, interest or development, and hence the document should serve as a vehicle for the diffusion of valuable knowledge and practice built up in schools.

Thirdly, I hope that by discussing the document some of the basic issues relating to the contribution of the subjects and disciplines to the humanities curriculum will be clarified, and that this, in turn, will enable people to design or amend their syllabi by giving consideration to a more appropriate disciplinary balance.

Fourthly, it is a matter of some concern that teachers should not follow the pattern that has developed in some secondary schools of a complete separation of the contributory subjects or even a separation of humanities from the rest of the curriculum. One would hope that, through the discussion of the matters reviewed in the document, relationships between humanities and other curricular areas, especially with mathematics, language, the sciences, and art and design, will be enchanced, and that areas of common concern will be identified.

Fifthly, there are problems of pupil assessment and course evaluation that are of concern across the curriculum and which affect the problems of monitoring pupil progress in all areas. It is hoped that this guideline document will encourage the consideration of a variety of necessary assessment procedures and will suggest some useful practices and principles related to course evaluation.

Sixthly, although the guidance on teaching techniques is implied rather than explicit in this document, nevertheless it should raise issues about the styles of learning developed in the schools and particularly the relationship between the styles of learning and the resources that are used.

Seventhly, it is important to consider the subtle mixing of all the constraints and opportunities that exist in curriculum design as they are related to the needs of children and their cognitive abilities at various ages. Particularly important are the special character of the disciplines as well as their common areas of concern, alongside the important questions of the resources available, not only in material terms but in terms of staff motivation, perceptions and skills. It is out of this subtle intermix of factors that go into the design of the curriculum that one would hope that a scheme or schemes can be devised that will simultaneously have intellectual rationality and coherence as well as the necessary basis of classroom practicability.

The proposals in this document are deliberately not set within particular age confines, as I believe it to be essential to consider the curriculum across a wider age range. Some forms of knowledge, skills and attitudes, are more appropriately developed in the early years, and others require the greater maturity associated with the upper school age range.

Although some of the ideas and issues presented here are 'my own', nevertheless, they inevitably represent ideas current in educational theory and practice which I have derived from a variety of published sources. More important than the formal sources are the considerable debts I owe to all those heads and assistant teachers in Northamptonshire schools, and to my colleagues in the Northamptonshire Inspectorate, for the discussion of the topics with which this document is concerned. I should also like to record the considerable help that I have received from members of Her Majesty's Inspectorate and colleagues working in other LEA's. The help that I have received is evident in much of the text and has been derived from lengthly discussion of ideas and issues, and the observation of classroom practices. The responsibility for the expression of the ideas and issues remains my own.

Chapter 1

Principles of Curriculum Design

A special feature of the humanities curriculum is that it is very close to life; whereas other areas of the curriculum may not have as their subject matter the concerns of people engaged in the complexities of everyday life and everyday social relationships, the humanities curriculum is essentially at the centre of our lives as social beings, and hence the issues raised about the humanities curriculum are those that are raised about the issues of political and social behaviour. Certain assumptions are made about 'worthwhileness' in any process of designing the curriculum in schools and of these it is necessary to be aware when we consider the humanities. 'Humanities' itself is a term containing inherent difficulties in that its definition varies from one side of the Atlantic to the other; 'the humanities' in North America is essentially that area of knowledge and human concern that relates to the 'high arts' and to the characteristics of civilization. So subsumed in humanities are, literature, painting, music, indeed all the fine arts, as well as the background context in which these studies are interrelated, that is of history. This is the definition taken by many universities, including the Open University. The term that North Americans would use for those studies that help to explain the social behaviour of human beings is, of course, social sciences, and here again it may be useful to look at the social sciences as a group of disciplines such as anthropology, sociology, psychology and, partially, geography, which are concerned with various aspects of the be-haviour of human beings in social contexts.

It is necessary to be clear about the interrelationship of the humanities and the social sciences. Humanities, in terms of its definition on this side of the Atlantic, and the one that is assumed in this document, consists of those fields of study and those disciplines that contribute to the understanding of human behaviour. One needs to determine what relationship the school curriculum has to humani-ties subjects even with this broad definition. A perusal of figure 1 will suggest that in fact the humanities or the social sciences are not part of the 'core' throughout, so that some of the subjects that contribute

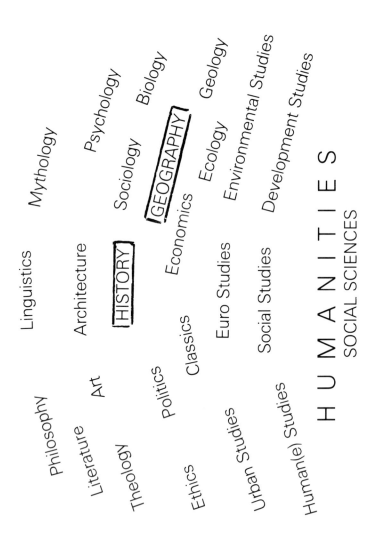

Figure 1

to humanities, such as history and geography, are established accepted subjects in the curriculum of most schools, particularly in those schools which have children from about the age of 8 through to the final school leaving age of 18. There are other subjects, such as economics and sociology, that are normally only taught in the upper secondary years.

There are other areas of study, and other disciplines, that are marginal to humanities, and which are shared with the natural sciences and with the studies related to linguistics. These are often the areas that are most characterized by growth and development, and often show the problems that 'the centre will not hold'.

When one looks at general assumptions about the nature of the curriculum, it is found that these can be divided into a number of categories:

(a) There are very basic assumptions about the nature of human beings and particularly that section of them whom we designate 'children'. Here we make assumptions not only about human psychology but also about what human beings are and their objectives, and so on.

(b) We make a number of assumptions about the aims of education. When these are discussed we may come up with rather bland definitions about education; for example, 'to make it possible for every citizen to enjoy fully the rights of a civilized life and to develop his cognitive and affective powers to the utmost limit, constrained only by his native ability and by the particular social and political environment in which he is living'. These aims would be seen by most of us as worthwhile but they are only of direct use when they are accompanied by deliberate strategies of learning.

(c) Related to these aims are assumptions about what it means to be educated, and here we face some particularly difficult problems about whether an educated person is the same as a person who has a great fund of knowlege, and what sort of knowledge would enable a person to be classified in the category of 'educated'. Would.this be someone with a high degree of specialized knowledge, or would an 'educated person', as an intrinsic definition, have an education that spanned a considerable range of human knowledge? One has to consider in exploring this question the 'data implosion'; it has been estimated that the sum of human knowledge is doubled, according to some experts every five years, by others every ten years. But it is reasonably safe to say that since the scientific and cultural revolution of the seventeenth century it has not been possible for any one person in his or her own lifetime, however talented, to have an appraisal of even the sum of human knowledge.

(d)   We make assumptions about the nature of knowledge and the relative value of different kinds of knowledge. This relates to the previous group of assumptions, but these are particularly concerned with some teasing questions about whether knowledge exists as an external entity in the sense that knowledge is an inherent part of the universe, and is there to be acquired, or whether knowledge is simply an artefact of human growth and behaviour? The assumptions that we make about the relative values of the different kinds of knowledge have been emphasized in the decades since 1945 by the arguments concerning the 'two cultures': whether it is more valuable to have an education which is largely based on traditional forms of study (mainly the arts and the humanities) or is the only valid form of knowledge in a world experiencing rapid technological change, a knowledge based on science and technology?

(e)   There are also crucial assumptions about society, as they are related to what we believe to be the good of the individual person and of human groups, and here we make a number of assumptions about the relationship of the education of the individual to the forms that societies take. One of the central issues in this debate is the classic discussion about education in society; that is, whether the schools should reflect society, challenge society or interact with society.

These assumptions about the curriculum in general have been set out because all of them reflect closely on our work in the design of humanities curricula, in that humanities touches on all these aspects of curriculum design in a way that not all other subjects and disciplines do. The matter of relating the learning process to the cognitive abilities of children of various ages has taxed the minds of a variety of academic specialists including psychologists, biologists and sociologists. This has proved a battleground between groups of people who have contributed ideas to this debate from a number of disciplines. Amongst the most influential theories have been those of Jean Piaget, whose ideas are complex and have been worked out over a very long period of time; basically his theories concerning conceptual development have tended to be interpreted as concerned with particular phases of cognitive development in children. The relevant phases for our purposes have been generalized as the following:

(a)   The *concrete operational phase*; roughly related to the age of most children between 7 and 11. In the concrete

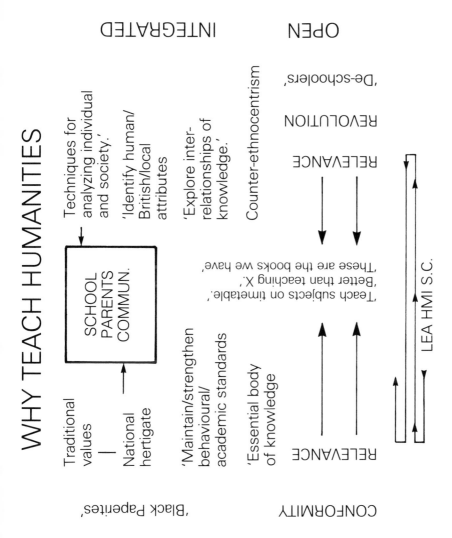

Figure 2

5

operational phase reasoning is tied to real objects and experiences.

(b) The *formal operational stage* which develops in most children from about the age of 12 onwards. Children increasingly make use of hypotheses and symbolic reasoning; that is they are no longer constrained by the surface appearance of reality but are increasingly capable of generalizing from a variety of experiences.

These two phases are preceded by earlier phases which are of less concern here, but it is noticeable that there will be many children who will in the later years of secondary school still mainly be thinking in a concrete operational context rather than in a formal operational context. The evidence from classrooms on this formal categorization suggests that this is a far from even development, and that one can see a great range of performance amongst any group of average children and one can see a great range of development in 'subject performance'.[1]

Another influential theory related to this is that of Jerome Bruner, whose work in the field of humanities has been a powerful influence on other people examining this curriculum area. Bruner's ideas were very influential in the development of the American scheme called MACOS — (that is 'Man: A Course of Study') — but from Bruner's contribution to the theories of learning, perhaps one of his most influential ideas is that of the *spiral curriculum*. This theory has had an enormous influence on the development of structure in learning and particularly on such contemporary theories as that of 'mastery learning'. Basically, the theory maintains that the curriculum should be characterized by the introduction of ideas at a simple cognitive level and a progressive reinforcement of the powerful concepts that form the structure of knowledge. In other words, the principle of selection of the content of the curriculum should be governed by the process of identifying the central ideas, and of reinforcing these over a long period of time as the curriculum is developed. So, essentially the subject matter will be valued by its conceptual power to develop cognitive growth. In the field of moral education important ideas have been developed by Lawrence Kohlberg, in that he has developed a theory of moral development and understanding which relates in some respects to the ideas of Bruner and Piaget about cognitive growth. Kohlberg describes a process in emotional and ethical growth which extends from conventional morality, which is simply concerned with obeying the rules, to that of the individual developing moral principles of his own; in other words, he has a sort of moral self-guidance system which is largely independent of immediate external constraints. Kohlberg's work is particularly important in the humanities because of the concern with developing standards and skills in the moral judgment of human behaviour.

A major issue in the humanities is that explored by researchers and educationists such as Liam Hudson who has produced a categorization of 'divergent' and 'convergent' thinking. Much of the teaching in humanities, as no doubt in the rest of the curriculum, is of teaching towards convergence of ideas and behaviour rather than that of stimulating creative imaginative responses. It is particularly important in the humanities, as it is so close to the development of moral, as well as of cognitive, understanding, that teachers should promote, encourage and value creative divergent thinking and unusual ideas, and above all help to develop in pupils techniques of constructive criticism. A great deal of deterministic patterning resides in the teaching of all subjects but perhaps the humanities, as they are so much concerned with matters of social and political behaviour, naturally tend to emphasize the conforming convergent lifestyle rather than the divergent, creative and perhaps sceptical approach to life.

When we come to the matter of the procedures to adopt in the selection of the content, there are a number of factors on which to consider and reflect. It is particularly important that we recognize that even in a society subject to slower social and technological change than Britain at the present time, it will be important to have most schemes of work and indeed, practices in curriculum design, in some 'self-destruct' form. It is extremely unlikely that one could devise a curriculum, particularly in the humanities in our own time, that should last indefinitely with only minor alterations. However, there are some basic factors which need consideration in devising a humanities scheme.

First of all, one might consider the social usefulness of the curriculum as it relates to the needs of pupils to understand the society in which they live, and to develop various skills, technical as well as social, that would help them to survive, to 'prosper', and to develop emotionally and cognitively.

Secondly, there is a need to develop a form of social awareness and responsibility, however we may interpret this. Widespread anxiety has been recently expressed about the responsibilities of schools for preparing pupils for life after school and also their need to respond to the expressed or implicit needs and demands of 'the community', whether 'community' is interpreted on a local on a national scale. The emphasis is that of response and interaction rather than of obedience and conformity, but nevertheless the clientele of the wider society needs more acknowledgement and regard than it has received in some schools.

Figure 3:   Curriculum Design ('Lawton Model' adaptation)

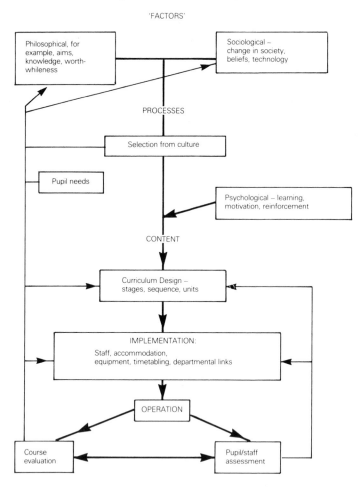

'FACTORS'

Philosophical, for example, aims, knowledge, worth-whileness

Sociological – change in society, beliefs, technology

PROCESSES

Selection from culture

Pupil needs

Psychological – learning, motivation, reinforcement

CONTENT

Curriculum Design – stages, sequence, units

IMPLEMENTATION: Staff, accommodation, equipment, timetabling, departmental links

OPERATION

Course evaluation

Pupil/staff assessment

Parental and social pressures, particularly as evidenced in some recent publications, notably the Taylor Report, suggest that the schools have a duty of accountability to the local, as well as to the national, community. It is highly significant that so much of the debate between the radical left and the traditional right, as exemplified in the 'Black Paper Era' of education, should be concerned with curriculum accountability, and also that so much of the 'exemplar' material should be cited from the humanities curriculum by adversaries on both sides of the debate.

Thirdly, there are so many minorities and 'variables' in any modern technology-orientated large-scale society that it is important to consider the implications of a 'common culture' and particularly the consideration that should be given to such matters as identifying some element of common beliefs and values. This issue has been enhanced in recent years by the development of Britain into a more ethnically and culturally heterogeneous society, and there are diverse opinions about the place of the 'New British' in our contemporary society. Whether we should regard the desirable pattern of development as that of a mosaic of different beliefs, values and lifestyles, or whether we should seek to achieve a more homogeneous society by some sacrifice of individuality for a 'common good' is a matter of personal belief, and one would hesitate to impose a uniform 'doctrine' on such a sensitive issue. Nevertheless it is of crucial importance that the issues relating to 'a common culture' are seen as live and significant.

Fourthly, there is the matter of the personal satisfaction of the students. One of the difficulties of the curriculum which is largely child-centred, is the intrinsic problem of children not necessarily being the most appropriate determiners of their own real needs any more than many adults are, and children conspicuously lack the dimension and diversity of adult experience. Ignorance of certain major areas of human knowledge undoubtedly operate as a powerful restraint on human development; hence the assertion by radical critics of education that the control of knowledge is the most effective form of political control.

Fifthly, cognitive development depends very much on the training of individuals in the understanding and development of analytical techniques, so that individuals need to have at their command a battery of concepts and techniques by which they can analyze not only society at large, but everyday phenomena, and be able to develop criteria for making judgments on individual and group behaviour.

Another central issue that we shall be concerned with in the development of the humanities curriculum is that of objectives in curriculum planning. As humanities is concerned with so much of life in school, as well as of life outside, it is particularly important that the objectives of the humanities curriculum are consonant with the overall aims of the school. Here it may be useful to look at the concept of objectives as statements of 'behaviour to be achieved after an element of learning has been acquired by the student'. This rather formal definition serves to emphasize the importance of differentiating between 'pre-specified behavioural objectives', in which the behaviour of the learner is seen as an individual who behaves differently at the end of a learning activity from the way he behaved before, and other learning objectives. The difficulty of pre-specified objectives is that although perhaps very useful for forms of instruction, particularly in areas of technical performance, their application in the field of humanities is likely to lead to an over-concentration on measurable specifiable outcomes, and hence to focus on those learning activities that are susceptible to forms of easily measurable or quantifiable learning. More relevant to the humanities curriculum are 'expressive intentions', which are those that describe educational encounters; they focus not so much on the outcome or the product of a learning process but on the learning process itself. The great advantage of thinking in terms of expressive intentions rather than of pre-specified instructional objectives is that the unpredicted developments and outcomes in a learning situation can be effectively allowed for. The danger of pre-specifying the curriculum too closely is that of emphasizing the peripheral rather than the essential and on limiting the initiative of the student. Perhaps of more importance is that pre-specified objectives imply a scientific clinical atmosphere in which children will go through robot-like processes of behavioural change, and, as all of us know, this is quite unrepresentative of the reality of life in classrooms.

One of the interesting aspects of objectives-based education is the utility of aims and objectives across a large part of the academic curriculum. If one looks at the strategy of the Schools Council Project 'Science Five to Thirteen' the central core of this is called 'With Objectives in Mind'; this shows, emanating from the central aim, that is of 'developing a system of enquiry and a scientific approach', eight other second level aims, all of which could be applied as much in the humanities as in the science curriculum. This illustrates the significance that should be attached to determining those objectives that would be preponderantly derived from specific areas of study rather than from the learning process as a whole.

So, in the case of specific objectives such as 'appreciating patterns and relationships', a number of subjects would contribute to the development of skills associated with this objective but they would contribute in different ways, so that the ecologically-minded scientist's study of animate or live matter in order to determine patterns of relationships, would be similar to, although not the same as, that of the sociologist, historian or artist.

One other matter that deserves close attention is the consideration of the whole curriculum of the compulsory years of schooling, that is from the age of 5 to the age of 16; if we take the 'messages' of both Piaget and Bruner concerning the sequencing and phasing of learning experiences, we need to determine which parts of learning are most effectively introduced and developed in each phase. Presumably, many skills and concepts would already have been developed in children before they reach the secondary school; hence it would be important to identify these, and to make sure that the learning processes were related to those developed in the early years. This calls attention to the crucial importance of effective liaison

Figure 4: Objectives for Children Learning Sciences (Schools Council Science 5–13 Project)

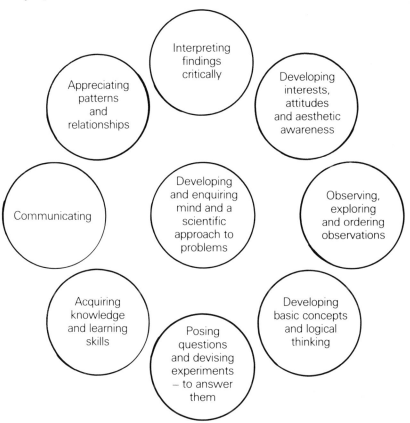

These objectives are as applicable in the newer approach to humanities and social sciences as they are in the natural sciences.

between schools. Sometimes the liaison is achieved (at the beginning) most effectively by the development of accurate pupil records. In other cases curricular coordination is most effectively attained by consultation between teachers in the different schools. Here, considerable work still needs to be done, particularly by the clarification of objectives in the related schools, and by looking at some closely-related matters such as pupil assessment procedures.

Important for the whole process of learning across the curriculum, as well as in the humanities, but not always given as much prominence in the humanities as in other subjects or disciplines, is the matter of enabling children to develop skills of learning. Study skills are developed over a long period of time but certainly all children should be taught how to develop a mode of enquiry and the associated reference skills of understanding how information can be stored, how it can be made accessible, the constraints that operate on certain types of information, and, above all, the idea of taxonomy and classification, so that information derived about an area of study through one discipline or mode of enquiry can be related to matters about the same field of study developed from other approaches to knowledge.

For the American High School Geography Project a basic learning-activity analysis was made in which it was stated that 'Students are asked to use cognitive skills/on data/to find generalizations/which illustrate important abstract ideas/which affect values and attitudes/and develop social skills.'

Note

1   See, for a brief discussion of Piagetian theory, books by P Richmond and D Boyle.

Chapter 2

Humanities in the School Curriculum

The Practice of Curricular Organization in Schools

There is naturally a great diversity of practice amongst schools in respect of both organization and curriculum; and these differences have been widely discussed. Some of the differences relate to the basic pattern of curricular organization and here one of the long-running debates has been on whether one of the roles of the year tutor, particularly in middle schools, is to determine the curricular pattern. The contrast is shown most sharply between middle schools that are organized on a conventional junior school basis, with the curriculum much influenced by the assumed needs of children, and the middle school with the conventional secondary subject-centred organization. Donald Moyle, in *The Reading Curriculum*, has suggested some fundamental differences, although these need to be treated with some reservation as essentially the differences reflect 'ideal' types rather than generalizations about actual schools.

	JUNIOR	**SECONDARY**
(i)	Broad orientation — to what is relevant.	Restricted. Broad developments may be non-academic.
(ii)	Integration is easy. It tends to be subjective; that is, based very much on teacher decisions, and functional, that is, it answers immediate perceived needs of children.	Integration is difficult and it is related to the specialist functions of teachers.
(iii)	Coherence of the subject is less important than the needs of the children.	Coherence is easy but this is pre-determined by the teachers who are disciplinary specialists.

(iv) Continuity is easy within the year. Teachers generally have flexibility in designing the programme and are less limited by subject boundaries, but consistency from year to year may prove very difficult.   Continuity within the year is difficult simply because of the fragmentation of the typical secondary school curriculum, but there is a consistency within the subject from year to year determined by the specialists.

(v) Teacher/pupil relationships are normally close but there is a considerable dependence on the knowledge of one adult, that is, the main class teacher.   There is a great diversity of teacher contacts and teachers may not know the pupils sufficiently well to use appropriate teaching and learning techniques.

In practical terms, in the vast majority of schools, there is not this polarization, in that most junior schools show some degree of specialization amongst the staff, even if this is mainly expressed in terms of teacher interest, and increasingly in secondary schools there is a measure of interdisciplinarity, particularly in the early secondary years. As in most education, indeed in all social processes, there are not sharp distinctions but a continuum. The continuum at one end is represented by an interdisciplinary form where the curriculum is seen as 'basic skills plus topics', or projects plus resource-based specialisms, for example, physical education, music, art and craft. At the other end of the continuum there may be excessive subject fragmentation, no longer visible in most schools, but many of us are familiar with secondary schools where English would have been commonly specified in categories of 'spelling', 'composition', 'grammar', 'literature' and 'drama'.

It is worth considering some of the curricular divisions that have been proposed by authorities on middle schools or on the middle years of schooling. The detailed references to these works will be found in the bibliography at the end of the document. The first that one might cite is that of Raggett and Clarkson when they write that 'Curriculum in the middle years in terms of the academic subjects could be classified in the following divisions:

(a) langugage, literature and drama
(b) mathematics
(c) science
(d) social studies
(e) modern languages'

Figure 5: Method of Enquiry

Notes

1 Scientists on 'research frontiers' behave more intuitively, think laterally, use serendipity.

2 Degree of uncertainty in scientific generalisation – fundamental change in paradigm model (see Kuhn, T S *Structure of Scientific Revolutions*).

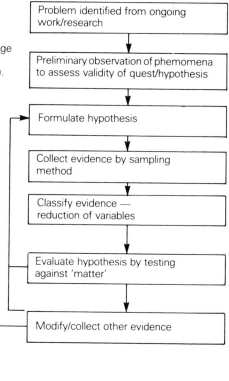

A tradition model of Scientific Method

Gannon and Whalley suggest the following five broad areas of study although they recognize the importance of interrelationships and of overlapping:

(a) 'language and communication'
(b) 'human and environmental'
(c) 'scientific and technical'
(d) 'creative and expressive'
(e) 'craft and practical'

Dennis Lawton, in his contribution to the BBC booklet on the *Middle Years Curriculum*, suggests a division in terms not so much of curricular areas but as forms of learning experience which relate to Paul Hirst's 'Forms of Knowledge':

(a) mathematics
(b) science
(c) humanities/social studies
(d) expressive and creative arts
(e) moral education

A sixth possible section is language although Lawton himself expresses considerable doubts about the teaching of modern languages in middle schools except as a taster for a possible development but not necessarily as a mandatory part of the core curriculum for all children. Moral education is seen not as a separate subject area but as a dimension of understanding that should infuse all other curriculum areas.

Other people writing and talking about the curricular divisions in the middle years have suggested even simpler classificatory systems, one being for example, investigative studies/projects/topics; in this sense investigative studies, largely concerned with the development of basic skills, would then be applied to projects, which are really areas of study pursued by the whole of a group although in different ways, and topics, those areas of study which would be closely developed by small groups of children or by individual children.

Fundamental disputes, and even confrontations, have developed around the issue of whether the determining factor in curriculum design should be the strategy of responding to the needs, however these are determined, of pupils, or whether the framework should be derived from the disciplines of knowledge. There are alleged to be strong advantages in a curriculum based to a large extent on pupil choice; these are the high motivation of the pupils, and the development of a great variety of reference skills and presentation techniques. The essential problems of pupil-determined learning, or learning where the pupils have a large measure of choice, are that one can end up with a form of 'serendipity curriculum' where children make chance encounters with crucial ideas. Particular problems are the lack of sequential development and the problems which teachers encounter in producing effective modes of assessment. The teacher-directed curriculum, characteristic of most schools, suffers from problems of stultification and 'remoteness' from the pupils unless it has a built-in responsiveness and flexibility. Most schools which are 'going well' tend to chose a 'middle stance' between these two extremes and seek for a balance of teacher-directed learning and of learning with an element of pupil choice. Most of us will recognize that there must be considerable contraints on pupil autonomy and that there are practical constraints in pupil and teacher knowledge related to the availability of, and accessibility to, appropriate resources. Some time has been spent on this issue of the contrasted elements of pupil choice and teacher direction because this is an issue of importance in many schools.

One of the objects of this document is to consider a possible framework for the humanities curriculum which is based on 'concepts, experiences and skills', which would allow more freedom of choice for the pupils and teachers, at least for some of the time, in determining the subject matter, but where the overall determination of the ideas and skills to be learned would be directed or would be determined by the teacher, or by teachers in collaboration.

It may help to refer to the ideas to which I subscribe in order to reveal some of the assumptions on which this text is based. I see the school subjects as abstracts mainly from the disciplines and from areas where the disciplines inter-react in a particular concern for exploring an area of knowledge. So in the humanities we could see history, geography, economics, sociology, psychology, anthropology as disciplines or forms of knowledge. Other areas are those fields of study where the disciplines interrelate, and these, as they relate to humanities, I would suggest are subjects such as politics and classics. These are essentially fields of knowledge; that is *areas of study* rather than *forms of knowledge*. Some subjects and disciplines are bridges between the natural sciences and the social sciences — particular examples of these are biology, particularly where there is an emphasis on social biology, and physical geography which is concerned with the natural environment in which human activities take place. One may consider a subject such as geography, which is essentially one of both the natural sciences, as it is concerned with studies related to the structure of the earth's surface and of the atmosphere, as also one of the social sciences, as geography is also concerned with human spatial behaviour.

It may also help to clarify the issue about subjects such as environmental studies. Environmental studies is perceived by me not as a discipline but as a 'field of interest'; it is really the study of a locality where a number of disciplines interact. The 'environment' is spatially defined and is investigated by the use of a combination of concepts and techniques drawn from a number of disciplines. The object of this combination is to explore a defined environment more effectively and thoroughly than would be possible by the approach of a single disciplinary specialist, such as a biologist, geographer or historian.

The last two decades have seen the growth of a number of 'fields of interest' such as 'European studies', which has often been used to support the learning of a modern language, 'development studies' or 'world studies', concerned with the relationships between the 'developed' and the 'undeveloped' world, and 'urban studies' which has been concerned with the characteristics and problems of cities and their inhabitants. A fourth area which is perhaps now gaining new strength, possibly related to the decline of the study of classical languages in schools, is that of classical studies, which originally developed as a contextual study for Latin and Greek, but now is broadening its concern to other ancient civilizations and with some crucial relationships in the humanities, particularly those with a 'natural interaction' such as mythology, literature and history. If one accepts the curricular divisions in schools as being five or six main areas of study, it is useful to consider those areas of concern which interact between humanities and other curricular areas.

1   *English*

(a)   'Language in its social context' has an emphasis on the understanding of communications media and a particular concern (bearing in mind the Bullock Report) with such matters as the audience for a communication and the social context in which the communication is made.

(b)   Drama has been underdeveloped in conventional history and geography teaching, although there is considerable opportunity for the development of empathy in exploring social relationships and in developing value judgments. Drama can give a heightened awareness of social behaviour and of important social issues; important recent developments in drama techniques allied to the analysis of human behaviour can give a depth of understanding not usually accessible through conventional classroom learning.

(c)   Literature is often related to young persons growing up and the encounters of children with the adult world. There is a wealth of literature which explores these relationships in the present and the past. Most of this literature is probably written with a juvenile audience in mind but one is conscious of the usefulness of novels and poetry which show children and adults in both strange and familiar environments. Examples of the sorts of literature that I have in mind would be a novel such as L P Hartley's *The Go Between* and William Golding's *Lord of the Flies.*

(d)   Mythology has been studied in one form or another in most schools so that it has been part of the reading programme of many children in junior schools and there is good material, both in books and audio-visual forms, concerned with the relationships between history and folklore. There are good opportunities for an exploration of the belief systems and superstitions of our own society compared with other societies both contemporary and historical. The mythology of the Ancient World is truly integrative in that studies can be based on the civilization of ancient Greece and Rome through the literature and mythology that has grown up about the classical past. If schools are to make a study of the relationships of myth, history and art in societies very different from our own, but also of societies with a considerable degree of complexity, then the classical world would seem to be the prime example of a suitable context.

2   Science

The basic concern of school science I would interpret as satisfying the needs of children to learn about, and to explore, the physical environment; this enquiry can be divided into three main categories:

(a)   A study of the nature of the earth's materials (here it has obvious links with geography). This is the area of study that Americans term the earth sciences and is largely concerned with physical geography and geology as well as with physics.

(b)   The study of forms of energy has links with humanities in its concern with the understanding and measurement of physical phenomena, especially the measurement of the atmosphere and the hydrosphere, and has also links with understanding of the historical development of technology.

(c)   The study of living organisms concerned with the important developing school subject of ecology which is concerned with the relationship between living organisms and the environment, and also with the understanding of 'ecosystems'; that is systems in which particular organisms interact. This has an important relationship with the study of the humanities, particularly where there is a strong environmental element in the studies. Particular concerns shared with the humanities would be those of primary production such as farming, fishing, forestry and so on, the study of human evolution, and the study of the relationships between human beings and the animal world.

Of special interest would be the development of an understanding of some of the concepts related to ecosystems; study of these sorts of ecological relationships, whether of plant or animal communities, is significant in understanding some of the human processes that have developed in both primitive and advanced societies. A major concern of ecologists, for example, is the study of the interaction of population and resources, and particularly the problems of populations that are symbiotically related to other groups and their dependence on resource systems which may operate fundamental constraints on development.

Perhaps the most significant of all the ideas to be taken from the science curriculum is that particular form of scientific enquiry which is normally called the 'hypothetico-deductive'.

This term simply refers to the 'traditional' scientific method with which we are all familiar: that is of first of all setting up a hypothesis; then of collecting evidence that would relate to this; of testing the hypothesis and accordingly rejecting it or provisionally accepting it; making a generalization, then searching for further evidence to extend the generalization. This method which was, in the past, particularly associated with the natural sciences, is largely applicable to the social sciences — in fact all those disciplines that deal with the complex matter of human behaviour. The crucial difference is that, except in the most extreme political contexts, human beings are not usually placed in a controlled hypothetical testing situation.

3   *Mathematics*

As science is most important for the humanities in illustrating the ways in which scientists work and in considering their methods of research, so there is a similar relationship between humanities and mathematics. The importance here is in the interpretation of logical relationships within systems and across systems. Particularly relevant for much of the work in modern geography is modern mathematics, especially where it deals with set and matrix relationships. An increasing amount of modern geography, economics and sociology, and more recently of history, depends on the analysis of quantitative data. Also important in reporting findings from these disciplines are the skills of interpretation and of the presentation of quantitative data in a variety of forms. A great amount of information that is gathered about human behaviour can be presented in a graphical form and more vividly by graphic pictorial presentation: of great significance for the interpretation of social and economic data is the rapid development of user-friendly computer graphics.

The mathematicians' continuing search for pattern, whether shown in the form of shapes, number or distributions, is of major concern to people working in the humanities field, and children lacking the appropriate mathematical skills will firstly be unable to search for the data, secondly be unable to evaluate its significance, and thirdly will find great difficulties in making an adequate presentation of the information derived.

Of considerable consequence to humanities are the great social changes that will result from the technological developments in advanced data handling and information processing. Although, as in so many of these widely canvassed changes resulting from develop-

ments in technology, the element of 'cultural lag' is often underesti-
mated or ignored, undoubtedly for many people the revolution in
data processing and the whole range of developments in micro-
electronics and in automated processes will have an important effect
on the working lives of many people. If one looks at the needs of the
people who will be adults in the twenty-first century, a major
omission in the school curriculum would be to have not prepared
children for an understanding of the social changes that are likely to
follow technological development. People need insights into the basic
technical processes involved in miniaturization and the advances in
data processing and control systems.

4 Concerns Shared with Art and Design

Humanities has important common concerns with art and design,
especially in the evolution and appraisal of the man-made environment; stimulating contrasts emerge from differing perspectives on the
artistic and mundane artefacts of our own and other cultures.

Art and design more closely than any other areas of the
curriculum, except possibly language, reflect most vividly the
conceptions and perceptions of particular cultures, so that if one looks
at the artefacts that emerge from the art rooms and design centres of
our schools, these reflect the way people in the latter part of the
twentieth century in Western Europe see their everyday lives in
their own societies. Cultures reflect particular social preoccupations
in what societies stress or ignore, and what aspects of reality are seen
as most significant and acceptable. If one took examples of this, one
would be particularly conscious of the importance of steam and iron in
Victorian Britain and the emphasis on the human form in ancient
Greece. Perceptions of variations in colour and texture are significant, particularly in what to English eyes might seem relatively
barren landscapes so that Eskimo cultures have many different terms
expressing the concept of 'whiteness', and desert nomads have many
different terms expressing the infinite gradations in the texture and
colour of sand. One of the most useful exercises for children to
perform is to adopt the 'Martian landing supposition' by envisaging
people from an alien society making appraisals of Western culture as
if from another civilization based on different preconceptions and
perceptions. This sort of exercise will be referred to again when we
consider the importance of extension studies for the most able pupils.

Humanities shares, with art and design, other concerns in
studying the technological development of societies and the cultural
artefacts that have been produced. One of the more significant
developments in twentieth century art has been the recognition of
the value and validity of the cultural artefacts of pre-literate or
non-literate societies; good examples would be from African and

Polynesian art. Of great interest is the cultural impact of the West, and particularly of mass production, on the art forms of non-Western societies. Very often this has resulted in the decay of artsitic form and the decline of the traditional skill of the artist in producing the object but, as the study of civilization is concerned with the rise of civilization and with its decay, there are obviously bonds between art and design on the one hand and the study of civilization in the humanities on the other.

Perhaps the most valuable relationships to be explored between art and design and the humanities are the practical applications of so many of the major human developments in creative technology. Effective cooperation between design teachers and humanities teachers can illustrate, in practical terms, some of the problems that craftsmen have had in dealing with particular materials — the actual processes of developing the technology that changed society. There are some design departments that can give useful observations and practical help in understanding what was involved in the technological changes of the early industrial revolution, or the development of the sailing ship, or of powered flight, and so on. A growing field of interdisciplinary cooperation is in the study of the urban built environment.

All of this leads to the necessity of giving adequate emphasis to coordination in curriculum planning. This does not imply an integration across very broad curricular areas, but a planning system by which, if we accept the Piagetian or the Brunerian phasing of learning by stages, and the necessity of building a sprial curriculum, then we must consider the logical order of the study units. Stages of development in humanities — for example the understanding of networks in geography — should be preceded by the appropriate stages in modern mathematics. If in the humanities department a study of ancient civilizations is about to begin, then this should, if possible, be related to work planned for the art department that is concerned with the art of the ancient world. What this implies is that there should be full consultation between the curriculum coordinators and that there should be planning to ensure that as far as possible there is an interrelationship and a sequencing of conceptual development related to study themes.

Some, if not most, difficulties relate to the social purposes of the curriculum and in this humanities has a particularly significant role to play. This is an extremely difficult area in respect of a number of factors which will be discussed elsewhere in this document, but here are two examples that seem particularly important.

Firstly, there is the issue of the values imparted in the humanities curriculum as they relate to people living in a multi-ethnic, multi-belief society. There has been a considerable amount of work which has emanated from bodies concerned with multi-ethnic education and in general one would conclude that there are particularly important perspectives concerned with living in a multicultural society, that should be developed in history, geography, the social sciences and so on. Very often this is not a matter of introducing special material but of developing the humanities curriculum in a more culturally-aware manner so that in cases of culture conflict it often helps to take the opposite of the conventional view in which so much of traditional British historiography seems to have the implicit assumption that non-European societies did not exist until they were discovered by Europeans. Similarly, the viewpoint taken on the British overseas is invariably that of the British settlers rather than that of the indigenous peoples and corrections and reinterpretations are necessary in these respects. British educational material, particularly in the humanities, is deeply infused with the ethnocentric cultural values, past and present, of our society, which is what one would expect; however there is a need to take account of varying cultural perspectives and to produce a learning system where children will be able to empathize with cultural groups other than their own.

Secondly, as the humanities curriculum presumably should reflect not only changing British society but changing British perceptions of the contemporary world and of the past, so one would look for a different sort of relationship between the formal school curriculum and the 'media curriculum' or, as the French term it, 'the alternative school'. This is a matter of considerable concern in the humanities because what may seem remote from 'the common culture' in some of the school curriculum is not so in the study of the humanities, any more than it is in a study of the English language.

A basic problem exists about the hidden curriculum and its relationships with the formal established curriculum. A number of observations here that I think pertinent are:

(i)   That what is set down in the curriculum does not very closely relate to what is actually transacted in classrooms in terms of pupils learning and teachers teaching, so that there is a gap, which it is well to recognize, between what purports to be the school's scheme of work in humanities or history or geography, or indeed in any subject, and what the children actually receive. There is a similar gap between the design of the scheme of work and the perceptions that the recipients or the clients have of the constituent parts of that scheme of work as well as of its overall rationale and content.

(ii) One should observe that, in the promotion of social attitudes and value judgments, the media are of enormous importance and that the place of the media in the lives of children, at least in the opinion of some authorities, is closely related to the level of attainment and education of the parents. This, one may conclude, provides us with a situation where children who are likely to be most persuasively affected by the messages that they receive from the popular media, particularly radio, television and the press, are those whose parents are least able to help them acquire critical responses and awareness. What seems to be a completely wasted effort is to try to seal children off from the effects of the media, particularly media that are obviously seeking to influence children in their social and commercial behaviour. Conspicuous amongst these, in influence, are children's comics and those programmes on television that secure large audiences of young persons.

As it would seem to be foolish and purposeless to try to remove the effect of the media, so it would be foolish and purposeless to base work directly on the presentation of the world and of social reality offered by the media.

It has been estimated that of boys in the age-range 9–13 something like two-thirds encounter a comic every week and a very high proportion of the 'comic' content sold to boys in this age range is concerned with historical and geographical matters. So much so that the two million comics, apparently concerned particularly with war-like matters, that are sold every week and which are read by, presumably, something like six or seven million children, are a major source of information about contemporary history and do much to mould children's perceptions of the contemporary world. Although the Second World War ended over forty years ago the war of the 'Anglo-Allies' against the Germans and Japanese continues to be represented every week in many children's comics.

The situation is rather different for girls, but not necessarily the less dangerous, in that girls would appear to graduate quickly from the *Beano* and *Dandy* level of the jovial and over-simple comic to the 'teenage romance' journal, or to the popular woman's magazine. Just as boys in the middle years are being fed with a diet, in many cases, of obsolete militaristic and ethnocentric attitudes, so the girls are being nourished with a distorted and over-romantic presentation of relationships between the sexes.

What is needed, is a curriculum policy which does not ignore the comic or the popular magazine and the popular television programme, but a policy which seeks to interact with popular culture. Popular reading and popular television (particularly with the aid of the video cassette recorder) should certainly not be ignored, nor necessarily deplored, but children should be trained to make an active, critical response and appraisal of the media diet which they are being offered. This is not so demanding as it seems; in fact a lot of the formal curriculum, as it will be set down in this document, does relate quite closely to what is being presented in various parts of 'non-school' curriculum, not only in the humanities but in the sciences, in health and sex education and undoubtedly in English and drama. To give children a battery of techniques and a basic conceptual understanding by which they can evaluate programmes by using criteria which one would hope that they would develop as adults, is not an insuperable task. Certainly one would hope that children can be made aware of the objectives of the media presenters, whether newspaper editors or television programme producers; can be made aware of the sort of market research that goes into the devising of programmes and 'presentations' either in printed media or audio-visual media, and can be given some insight into the world of public relations and advertising and into those complex strategies by which 'consent is engineered'. This policy is not separate from the rest of the curriculum; in fact, one of the healthiest developments visible in many schools is that of children learning techniques of criticizing the material that they use in school. It is compatible with the whole approach towards evidence in the learning process. As we hope that children will learn to comparatively evaluate evidence and make value judgments on the basis of material that they encounter relating to historical, geographical, environmental and social topics, so one would reasonably expect that these skills of critical appraisal can be transferred to the whole of popular culture.

I am not suggesting that popular culture in itself is bad or to be ignored or treated condescendingly. There is much of value in the world of popular music and of the comics, particularly in the lively presentation of events and personalities. There is much that appears on television that is apparently not related directly to education but, nevertheless, is of considerable educational value; one need only consider the value of the study of the social ethics presented in so many American animated cartoons or of the social values incorporated and embalmed in the most popular television 'soap opera' serials.

These two issues, that of learning to live in a multi-ethnic society and of learning to interact effectively with the popular culture, are simply selected as particular examples of those areas where the curriculum needs to relate much more closely to the world of reality. It is necessary to make the formal curriculum recognize, at the least, and, at the best, interact with, the hidden curriculum with which most children's consciousness is infused.

Chapter 3

The Contributions of Disciplines to Understanding Human Behaviour

In this 'guideline' the disciplines are seen as resources for the interpretation and understanding of human behaviour. This is not to suggest that in school all human behaviour can be understood, but that children will develop basic ideas and insights which are to be gained by the application of the skills and concepts of particular disciplines and also learn of the constraints that similarly limit understanding. The pattern of the units described will show a variation from some units where a number of disciplines or fields of study will be involved, to others (the majority of these are in Phase Three and Phase Four) which are essentially one-subject or one-discipline studies.

'Disciplines seen as resources' implies that the disciplines, or school 'subjects' in a conventional sense, far from being less important in interdisciplinary schemes, are effectively more important. They not only provide particular ways of 'seeing', and particular interpretations that interrelate with the perceptions and interpretations of other disciplines, but also in many cases the ideas and techniques of one discipline are used alongside the ideas and techniques of another discipline, and serve to heighten awareness, not only of the common ground shared by a number of disciplines, but also the highly individual character of these particular forms of knowledge. With this approach to the humanities there are considerable problems in determining the subject matter of the units of study.

Certain assumptions have been made about the units of study in the process of selecting the thematic material.

Firstly, the units of study, which in turn relate to the thematic material, need to be related to the perceived needs of the children and to their levels of conceptual understanding. Reference was made in the previous chapter to the fact that, although one might accept the sequential stages of conceptual development particularly associated with the work of Piaget and his disciples, nevertheless one would expect an enormous range of conceptual development in any group of children of the same chronological age. This matter of relating the material to children's development can be set against the necessity for providing units of study that are adaptable to the *needs* of the most intelligent and the most cognitively skilled children, as well as those of the children who have difficulties in coping with the work produced for children of average ability.

Secondly, there is a need to consider the structure of the disciplines themselves as their concerns are expressed, the way that specialists in the disciplines operate, and the way their researches are presented; these factors will determine what sort of subject matter is accessible to the approach of a particular discipline or group of disciplines.

Thirdly, the resources available must have a major determining effect on the subject matter selected in that there were a number of errors of judgment, as they appear in hindsight, that can be observed in the selection of rather esoteric resource material for some earlier Schools Council projects. In times of limited resources and falling numbers of pupils in the schools, it is important that the themes selected for study can be adequately resourced within existing school budgets or with only limited additional expenditure.

Fourthly, little is said in this document about learning methods, although it is hoped that for each of the themes some recommendations will be made by teachers about the appropriate learning methods to use with the individual units concerned. The author takes the view that there should be a great diversity of learning techniques, so that in any one unit one might well find a formal lesson for a whole group in introducing a particular theme (although this formal lesson would often be accompanied by a 'presentation' using some form of audio-visual equipment) to other elements in the unit where the work would characteristically be that of individual children or of small groups.

Fifthly, there should be an overall coherence in the system, so that the course will show lines of development and strong co-ordination below the superficial outlines of the unit themes; this coherence will relate particularly closely to the structure of the disciplines and to the Brunerian ideas of spiral, sequenced conceptual development.

When these considerations are borne in mind we finally come to the crucial question of what Professor Dennis Lawton has called a problem of 'selection from the culture'. Here we are to encounter difficulties in terms of the highly idiosyncratic individual perceptions of what is important, not only in our contemporary view of reality, but also of what children will need to know in another twenty or thirty years. This selection is a demanding task for teachers and is more effectively done by discussion in groups because there is inevitably an element of uncertain prediction and a problem of striving for compatibilities that may be difficult to attain. All of us are aware of the difficulties that many parents face in understanding modern curricular developments in schools, whether of the learning of a foreign language or an understanding of modern mathematics or science, and so on. Hence it is important that there is a justification for all of the units in a form that the children can understand, their parents can understand, and which could be generally justified to the community at large. Undoubtedly the major problem is in making a feasible 'crystal ball' projection into what are the likely scenarios for the national future. At one extreme we have a scenario based on a national model of high consumption and mass production by an intensive, technically highly-skilled labour force with extensive leisure opportunities and pursuits; this sort of society presumably would be characterized by a great deal of creative diversity in lifestyles and occupations, but bringing in its wake a host of new as well as exacerbated existing social and psychological problems.

The alternative extreme scenario is of Britain as an economic and social entity characterized by low productivity, large scale unemployment and with great extremes of affluence and poverty, so that alongside the minority of very affluent people there would be continuing unemployment and poverty for a large part of the community. The increased leisure may in fact be enforced leisure as the result of unemployment and job displacement resulting from technological developments, and of limited growth or decline in major occupational areas. We may be envisaging a small highly-skilled workforce in some manufacturing and in many service industries, backed by a large number of low-skilled, employed workers with marginal employment security, with an increasing number of people engaged in welfare and in administrative and social 'maintenance'. Presumably the national future will be somewhere between these two extremes, but it would be an important part of the education of all children by the time they reached school leaving age to have become aware of possible alternatives in national development.

There is a considerable amount of work on record about the problems of selecting many of the basic issues that should be explored by the school curriculum. Some of the more celebrated research has been associated with Jerome Bruner and Peter Dow, particularly in the background thinking to the American project entitled 'Man — A Course of Study'. The main questions pursued by the educationalists working on this project were the following:

(a)   What is specifically human about human beings?

(b)   Why do individuals and groups differ from one another and in what ways?
(c)   How do individuals and societies make decisions and ensure their implementation?
(d)   How do ideas evolve in human groups and how are these ideas diffused?
(e)   What factors influence human social and technological development?

It would be absurd to expect that children at school are going to find completed answers to these questions, but presumably most of us would accept the basic premise that, in the case of this socially-orientated area of the school curriculum, the pursuit of the enquiry is at least as important as the achievement of a final destination. As the final destination is 'unattainable' in the case of each of these problems, it is the strategy of the search that is particularly important; most of the study units will go some way to answering a number of these questions or at least have a focus that will bear on one of them, or on other crucial issues about human experience and behaviour that are not contained within these questions.

More consideration will be given to the contributions of the main disciplines involved in the humanities in later chapters, but enough has already been suggested to indicate that many of the developing areas, in relation to the study of these aspects of human behaviour, are areas of concern common to a number of disciplines. So if one looks at figure 6 which shows some of the developing areas as between geography on the one hand and history, economics, sociology and the natural sciences on the other, one can see that many of the themes relate to areas of common concern or where there is a 'natural' implicit need to use the concepts and techniques of more than one field or form of study. This figure has deliberately placed geography at the centre. It would be quite as appropriate and quite as logical to place the natural sciences at the centre, or history, or sociology, or economics, or literature. Geography has been selected in this case as its character has so often been cited as that of a bridge between the natural sciences and the social sciences or humanities. Geography shares common concerns with the natural sciences, particularly in that area which is described as the earth sciences, and shares with history a concern with human behaviour, particularly in its concern with the development of communities and the changing face of the landscape. Geography shares with economics an interest in particular forms of human spatial behaviour and systems related to production and consumption. It shares with sociology particular concerns with the social roles and functions of human beings and the

Figure 6: Geography — some interrelationships with other curriculum areas

(i) This diagram only suggests some of the relationships with other subjects.

(ii) 'Natural sciences' subsumes a number of subjects.

(iii) These curriculum areas have relationships with one another which are not indicated

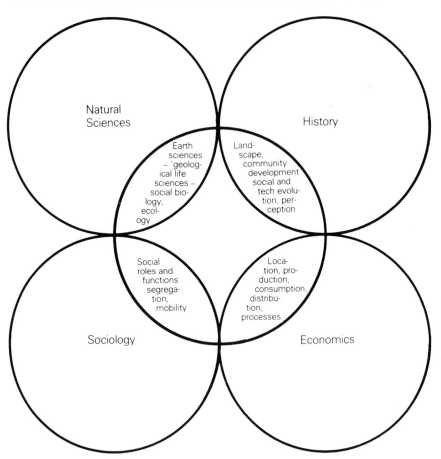

way these are exemplified or represented by spatial distributions.

It may help to clarify the relationships between the disciplines by considering two particular units, one from Phase One, which we might identify with the middle years of the primary school, and one from Phase Four, which might equally be interpreted as appropriate for the upper secondary years.

Phase One Unit I

'The Individual and the School'

This is the first unit suggested, although it would not necessarily be in any fixed order in relation to other first phase units. Essentially it is a predisciplinary unit, so it might well be tackled in some form in the early years, perhaps with eight-year-olds or with nine-year-olds. If one wished to use this theme as a vehicle for introducing the disciplines, one could produce sub-units that showed in an elementary form the particular ways that disciplines could contribute to the understanding of an institution which may be observed at close hand.

As an historical approach one might study the evolution of the school from its origins, the age of the parts of the building, use records of the past such as school log books or diaries, and study its changing character, changing teaching methods and resources. A geographer, looking at the school, would probably be particularly concerned with the school and its catchment area, the relationship of the school buildings to the immediate locality the school in relationship to transport systems and to social and community facilities, and perhaps to develop the idea of functional zones within the school and the idea of patterns of movement. A sociologist studying the school might analyze its hierarchies and its functional divisions by age and sex in the use of facilities, the responsibilities of the teaching and other staff, the particular groupings that were used for various forms of learning, and the pattern of organization of the school day. An economist would be interested in its running costs and the breakdown of the elements of the cost of maintaining the system, viewing the school as a sort of input/output model of supplies and equipment going in and, presumably, the output of educated children and psychologically-rewarded teachers at the 'production' end of the system.

A very similar procedure could be applied in studying a local shopping centre, in that the geographer's perspectives would be mainly concerned with the location of the centre and the movement of the people, the relationship between the centre and the residential patterns of the consumers using it, and with the suppliers who maintained it; the historian would be concerned with the evolution of shopping patterns and changing shopping styles; the sociologist would be interested with the dimensions of consumer behaviour and in 'patterning' by class, age and sex; the economist would be concerned with matters of rent and output, productivity and profit.

These examples of disciplinary specialists interacting in the exploration of institutions or systems are given as examples of high-level interdisciplinary cooperation; their equivalent in junior school enquiry would obviously be more concerned with 'ways of seeing' than with the application of advanced concepts.

A Unit from Phase Three

'History/Geography. Industrial Location Factors in the Early Technological Era in North and Central England.'

This is a good example of a unit where historical, geographical and economic factors are all closely associated and where one would certainly need the interpretations of more than one discipline to give a satisfactory and sufficiently detailed account of the processes that need to be described and understood. The historical aspect would be the application of mechanical power to production, with the evolution from direct water power, derived from stream locations, to the use of coal power and the developing technology of steam. With this would be associated the study of the mass production of important materials, specifically iron and later steel, and the transformation of these materials by industrial processes. Apart from the studies in the development of industrial processes, one would hope to find some help, not only from museum visits to examine the particular technology, but also, perhaps, from those concerned with the teaching of technology in schools. The important studies from the historical point of view would be the social results of changing technology and the consequent rapid urbanization, particularly in some areas of Britain. It is here that the concerns with the social effects of industralization in the early years of the Industrial Revolution would invite the consideration of a great variety of evidence. If this can be applied to the local area as well as to the more 'important' areas in a historical sense, then this would be of considerable benefit to the student pursuing this theme.

The geographical aspect would be concerned with industrial location factors and the spatial development of the urban areas. Particularly important in the location of the early industries were the source of power, access to raw materials, the development of transport systems, the transport and market hinterland, and what in American terminology is called 'the labour field'. This might well have another dimension by linking with other units to examine the problems of rapid urbanization in other parts of the world. Basic economic ideas would be an integral part of the study in that there would be strong evidence of a further and more fundamental division of labour, the importance of the accretion and distribution of capital through the financial system, and the allocation of resources for development. Sociologists are interested in the effects of concentrating large numbers of people near the bases of production and share with historians a concern with family life and the effects of these developments on the social class system. Political studies would be concerned with government regulation or lack of regulation, the growth of political power of the owners of industry in this era, and with governmental intervention in the form of factory and housing legislation. Other features related to the study of these issues would be the increasing pressure for more adequate popular representation in the government, and in the representation of labour interests in industry. It is notable that there is no clear-cut division here between the concerns of the disciplines, although each discipline would have particular methods of approach and particular resources and particular forms of presentation of the evidence. It is also notable that there would be an inevitable reliance on the cognitive development of the students in other curricular areas, particularly in science and technology in undestanding the application of mechanical power of production, and of mathematics in obtaining a measure of the changes that were taking place whether in the production of materials or from the increase in population in particular localities. Of major importance would be the evidence that is available for the changes that took place and on matters of causation, that is, the reasons for developments at particular times and in particular places.

A similar approach could be applied to virtually any of the units, even those which would seem to have an overwhelmingly one-subject or one-discipline base, where it would be necessary to consider the contribution of ideas and insights that could be provided by other disciplines or fields of study. We might well consider this in a unit which would seem to have a one-disciplinary implication; for instance, the study of political revolution, where suggested examples are revolutions in France, Russia and China. If the Russian Revolution were particularly selected for study in depth, then it would be necessary to study not only the history of Russia before the twentieth century, but also the geographical character of Russia including the great problems produced by the characteristic extremes of the Russian climate, and by the enormous distances, together with the associated problems of the underdeveloped technology of transport at that time. Similarly one would need to investigate some of the political ideologies of the main groups of people involved, as well as the distribution of social and economic power in Russia in the early twentieth century.

The assumption is made that from Phase One to Phase Four there would be increasing subject or disciplinary specialization; units are far more likely to be susceptible to subject labelling by the end of the middle years than at the beginning. It may help at this stage to look at some basic ways of seeing the contribution of any discipline or subject to the humanities curriculum. More consideration will be given to this in later chapters, but fundamentally we might take the example of history and consider two main interpretations of it.

Firstly, there is what one might call the 'treasure trove' approach to history; that is the fundamental question posed is 'What do we know of the past?' Learning is essentially about the subject matter of history; 'What happened in the past?' as a matter of largely uncontroversial record. The second approach is one that we might call 'enquiry method', and this has as its basic question 'How do historians find out about the past?' Related to this are the sub-questions 'How do they present their evidence?' and 'How is it that the views of historians on the past conflict?'

It is necessary to draw attention to the importance of the 'ideas linkage' between the units. One of the essential difficulties about the selection of material that is determined, not by conventional systems such as chronology in history, or world topography in geography, is that of making the relationships between the units clear both to teachers and to pupils. In geography one is concerned with concepts and skills related to spatial patterns, whether in the features of the surface of the earth or in the location of human activities and the spatial relationships between human communities. In history, one is concerned with particular types of experience that human beings have encountered, or historical experiences that raise crucial issues either about the nature of history itself or about the relationship of history to other disciplines. My own assumptions about this procedure of selection by concepts, skills and experiences, rather than by conventional taxonomies of chronology or topography, are that it is essential to have 'classificatory artefacts'. I have used this term to suggest all those systems or taxonomies that relate subject matter in conventional ways, so in geography one is immediately concerned with the spatial location of people and of environmental features on maps on a variety of scales, and in historical experience, the identification of historical events and personalities on a series of time lines, again presented on a variety of scales. Further discussion of this matter is developed in the chapter on resource material.

The concept-based curriculum is related to extending and enriching often quite simple ideas, but this extension and enrichment is entirely dependent on the approaches to a variety of material that is learned by the pupils, whether this material is conceived in the form of visual or written presentations, or artefacts of fieldwork.

Humanities is important, not only in the cognitive development of children, but also in their evolving attitudes to human beings in their social context and in the development of appropriate criteria for making value judgments. The key questions which are tackled by the humanities disciplines are important, not for finding solutions to fundamental human problems — in fact most of these are 'insoluble' — but in understanding the fundamental structure of issues; for example, in evaluating the validity of arguments for and against motorway construction, or in comparing the objectives of rival political interest groups, in order to learn to make judgments on a great variety of human issues wherever there is a conflict of human interest or of interpretation. Many major concepts and experiences relevant to humanities are often associated with social science subjects not represented in the curriculum for the middle years or even for the secondary years. I would select as of crucial importance a number of concepts taken from disciplines such as anthropology, sociology and psychology. Some of these are related to quite sophisticated approaches that are appropriate for a developed formal operational stage of understanding, but others are so basic to an understanding of human behaviour that they cry out for a place in the curriculum for children in the secondary years.

Two examples should suffice at this stage, although there are others that would need to be considered as they relate to the central ideas which are encountered in the study units. The first example is that of the 'culture concept', which is a basic interpretation used by social anthropologists. It is essentially a concept that illuminates the relationship between human beings and their environment, so that 'the culture concept' will be fundamental in explaining why, for example, the status and role of women and elderly people differs so much from one society to another. It also illuminates the relationship between art and community, and of technology as a part of a community's expressive life. The 'culture concept' illuminates many of the basic situations and experiences that children will encounter in history and geography. If one takes 'culture' as that whole range of behaviour and understanding by which human groups tackle the problems of survival and of the explanation of life, then one is close to the heart of the matter. At a more limited level this concept will explain, for example, why the approach of two groups to very similar environments will be completely different. This is often largely interpreted as related to technology, but behind this technology is a cultural perception of what is the interactive stance between the human beings and the environment with which they are faced. Good examples of this would be the similarities in the natural vegetational and climatic environment of areas such as Morocco and Arizona, and the complete contrast in the ways in which these areas have been developed and of the lifestyles of the inhabitants of these regions.

A second example of crucial ideas in social sciences that have much bearing on history and geography are those derived from sociology. One group of ideas is built around 'community' as contrasted with 'association'. 'Community' embodies the idea of intrinsic membership where people are bound together by ties of kinship or by perceptions of traditional 'inherited' common interests. So we can find 'communities' best expressed in the modern world in those small groups of people who live in relatively defined environments. One can realistically talk about 'community' as applying in 'villages', although these may be 'urban villages' as well as 'rural villages'. 'Communities' bind people together in something more than matters of passing interest or concern. Contrasted with 'community' is the idea of 'association', where people relate for specific purposes and in a more limited way, and this is, of course, a characteristic of many of our great metropolitan areas where individuals may perform a variety of roles. These roles imply limited 'associations', so that a 'community sense' in a suburb may be considerably lacking, although this is not necessarily so. This basic concept of 'community and association' is of great significance in interpreting social change in the modern world and particularly in understanding the effects of large-scale aggregations of human beings in urban areas.

Similar groups of concepts from the social sciences that may be of great importance in illuminating aspects of the behavioural studies in the humanities are concepts such as 'social class' and 'roles and functions', and those related to conflicting perceptions of environment and social reality.

It is necessary for all of us to be aware of our own internalized framework of perceptions. If one talks to groups of people working in the humanities are concepts such as 'social class' and 'roles and particular perception of the humanities related to their own area of special interest or to their own particular educational experiences.

Some of the more obvious perceptual frameworks (see table 1) are the following:

Table 1: Frameworks for Selection

(A) Topographical/regional:
British Isles, Western Europe, Southern Continents, North America
Developed ⟵——————⟶ Undeveloped
(B) Chronological:
Earlyman/ancient civilization/mediaeval/early modern/contemporary/future
(C) Environmental Scalar:
Locality/urban area/region/country/world
(D) Conceptual/thematic
Survival/power/organization/communication
(E) Community/settlement
(F) 'Functional Man, Woman'
(G)
(H)

(a)   The topographical/regional: people tend to design a curriculum which shows a pattern concentrating on the British Isles and then takes, regionally, the major areas of the world; or another topographical regional framework may suggest a classification based on 'First World', 'Second World' and 'Third World'.

(b)   Another framework is the chronological one where all of the humanities experiences are related through a time perspective which starts with the evolution of 'man' and continues through to the contemporary world. Expressed in some forms it may lead from Palaeolithic woman to Mrs Thatcher, or it may lead from cave illustration to 'painting by computer'.

(c)   'The environmental-scalar' perception is a relatively more recent form; this tends to see the world of the humanities as expressed in a series of increasingly complex ecological environments.

(d)   Another conceptual framework is that of the 'social-thematic' approach dominated by great overarching concepts such as 'survival', 'power' and 'communication'.

(e)   Popular in many primary schools is that of the functional personal classification which has such unit titles as 'Man, the Toolmaker', or 'Woman, the Housekeeper' and so on.

That is not to suggest that there is anything wrong in these perceptions, except perhaps in some cases for the 'sexist' implications. The important thing for teachers and children is to have an awareness of these particular frameworks of apprehending reality in order that they may make the necessary corrections to attain a balanced curriculum. It may help in many cases for us to come forward with a straightforward declaration of our interests.

Perhaps the most dangerous of all these perceptual frameworks is the one which insists that all human life can be adequately observed from the immediate environment of the school. Although impressive work has been done in this area, it is important to be aware of Bertrand Russell's caveat of the 'tyranny of familar surroundings over the imagination'.

There are problems in the practical definition of humanities in schools; in practice the term may comprehend:

(a)   History and geography taught as separate subjects.

(b)   History, geography and religious studies taught separately.

(c)   History, geography and religious studies combined in an interdisciplinary form, at least for some of the years, although they may be separated in others.

(d)   History, geography, religious studies and others, for example, politics and classics, which again may be taught in an interdisciplinary mode for some years but are more readily separable in others.

(e)   Humanities may find its main outcome in the form of environmental studies, which in some schools is linked with science.

(f)   Humanities may be presented in the form of environmental studies, but here generally not linked with science.

(g)   Humanities may be closely related to English or other subjects on a thematic or content basis.

Figure 7:   Major Themes in History and Geography

| Planet earth — evolution, landscape, climate | Human evolution and survival | Population and settlement |

F R A M E W O R K S

| Primary industry — farming, fishing, mining | Sources of energy and technology | Secondary industry manufacturing — |

T E C H N O L O G Y

| Communication of ideas and information | Movement of people and materials | Urbanization and its consequences |

M O V E M E N T

| Political and social ideas — conflict and cooperation | Religious beliefs and institutions | Leisure, recreation, culture |

C I V I L I Z A T I O N

Chapter 4

Geography in the Humanities Curriculum

It is not proposed in these brief chapters in the document to give an account of the changes in the main humanities subject areas because this task has been very well performed in a number of texts that are cited in the bibliography, but briefly those people needing a more detailed interpretation of what school geography is about, and what the present perceptions of the structure of the subject is, are advised to consult Norman Graves (1979) *Curriculum Planning in Geography* as probably the most up-to-date synthesis of recent development in this subject area. There are a number of other important books that give a good indication of the development of geography in the secondary school which are cited in the bibliography.

As in all the subject areas of the humanities curriculum, one must look to the contributory disciplines first of all to find out the appropriate learning concepts and skills to extract from them in order to develop the relationships with the other 'factors' that have been discussed in the previous chapter. In some curricular areas there is an implicit definition by title which allows us to discriminate between the school subject on the one hand and the intellectual discipline on the other, so that 'social studies' may be seen as the abstract from the 'disciplined' structures of the social sciences which has been appropriately modified and adapted for a school learning situation. Geography is not usually distinguishable in this way, although there are times when it may be more useful to talk about what is learned in classrooms as geographical studies rather than as geography, in the sense that it is difficult to find much correspondence between geography as it is taught in many schools and what geographers actually do in universities and other institutions of higher learning. It would not be difficult to produce a quick, but bland, description of the changes that have come about in geography in the last twenty years, but people interested in this have a plenitude of literature with which to refresh their own knowledge of these considerable movements.

In general one might say that geographers have moved towards a more systematic analytical approach, away from a descriptive approach based on the map and on the written account. A professor of geography some twenty years ago said that his subject should be conceived of as a 'light in the mind rather than as a load on the memory' and this is the fundamental approach that is shown in much recent geographical work. If one asks, 'What do geographers do?', then the answer can be a very long one or can be reduced, perhaps, to a superficial level, but basically their preoccupations are concerned with the analysis of spatial patterns in order to understand how the features of the earth's surface, and the inhabitants of the earth's surface, are located and how they interact. Mainly we are studying processes and systems. Some basic overarching concepts in modern geography are the following:

(a) 'Location' — the position and distribution of both living creatures, particularly human beings, and the inanimate features of the Earth's surface. Beyond this is the analysis of the association of functions; research is concerned with why particular functions or groups of artefacts or living creatures are related to particular places.

(b) 'Interaction' — this is interpreted as the relationship between human beings and their environment, although this interaction may be extended to a concern with the relationship between any living creatures and the natural 'inanimate' environment. Basically, this follows an older pattern that would have been familar in the interpretation of geography in the first half of the twentieth century: its concern was with the cultural and technological response of human beings to the survival problems posed by the natural environment.

(c) 'Distance' — 'distance' is interpreted much more widely now than it would have been in the past, so it is concerned with the relationship between distance and time which implies an understanding of those parts of the technological apparatus by which people organize themselves in societies. 'Distance' is also about the geometry of route efficiency in the sense of determining what is the most effective network of communications to overcome the 'friction of distance'.

(d) 'Scale' — 'scale' is interpreted not only as the manner in which reality or an abstraction from reality is represented, but also as the related problems of comparative scale; that is from small isolated units to very large aggregations of functions, people or artefacts.

(e) 'Change' — much of modern geography is preoccupied with the problems of spatial change in the sense that geographers are concerned with how ideas or technologies are diffused or applied to patterns of sequent occupance, in which one group occupies an area previously occupied by a different and perhaps less 'ecologically suitable' group. Geographers are also concerned with the processes by which individuals, and also large and small human groups, change in their locational associations.

Of the various conceptual frameworks in geography which claim attention at the present time, the one that is perhaps the most relevant geography to school learning is the 'Ecosystem' framework. This can be sub-divided into a series of systems and one could say that the object of learning geography is to gain an insight or induction into the way these systems operate:

(a) The Climatic System is concerned with the measurement and understanding of the patterns indicated by the weather and with the ways of representing the climatic system.

(b) The Geomorphic System is concerned with the physical features of the earth, including its landscape and scenery, and the long-term processes of change. Even though the Geomorphic System may appear in everyday terms to be static, in fact there is a constantly changing relationship amongst the 'plates' which make up the surface of the earth, and with changes in the hydrosphere.

(c) The Biotic System is concerned with vegetation and soil which in interaction with the climate has produced what traditional geographers have termed 'natural regions'.

(d) The Agricultural System is concerned with the whole variety of farming and farming systems, especially the

Figure 8:   Key Geographical Ideas

LOCATION — Accessibility, Distance, Interaction
SPATIAL DISTRIBUTION — Places/People — Patterns
MOVEMENT — 'Migration, Hierarchy, Convergence, Succession, Diffusion,
            Sequent Occupance, Distance Decay'
TYPICAL 'CONTENTS' FOR MIDDLE YEARS AGE GROUP
1   LOCALITY ⟨— Farming, Rural Society
                 LAND USE, WORK
                 Industry/commerce, Urban Society
    'DECISIONS', 'CONTINUUM'
2   OTHER ENVIRONMENTS:— 'Compare and Contrast'
    A)   Community Emphasis — Basic Needs; Environment Issues
    B)   Man and Natural Environment — Soil, Climate
    C)   Patterns of Change: for example *Technology, Vegetation, Politics*
    D)   Decision-making Process — Evidence; Judgment values
    — Alternative Choices
    Use of MODELS, SIMULATIONS

Figure 9: *Geography Concept Clusters*

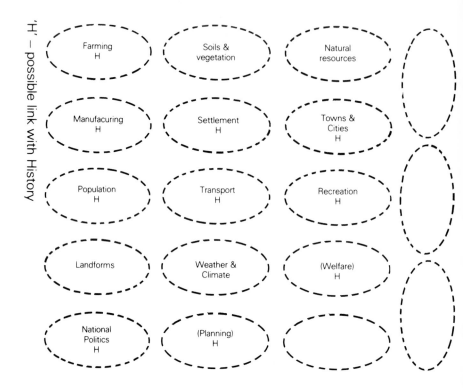

production of crops of all sorts and with stock-rearing. Related to this system are processes that are concerned with using the products of the sea.

(e) Manufacturing Systems are concerned with the principles and practice of industrial location and with sources of material and of power.

(f) Settlement Systems can be divided into three groups:

    (i) population — concerned with the distribution and aggregation of population and its dispersion;

    (ii) settlement — concerned with patterns of land use, and with settlement growth, functions and hierarchies;

    (iii) networks — concerned with movement between and within settlements and with patterns of accessibility.

The geographers of Her Majesty's Inspectorate produced in the summer of 1978 a very useful publication called *Teaching of Ideas in Geography* where they used a classification that was more closely related to the school system than to the functional divisions in academic geography. The systems which they used in order to explore central geographical ideas are the following (see also table 2):

(a) 'Farming' — types of farming, marketing of products, specialization in farming regions;

(b) 'Land Forms' — landscape processes, erosion and landscape evaluation;

(c) 'Manufacturing' — location, industrial inertia, agglomeration and classification;

(d) 'Natural Resources' — the environment and resource evaluation;

(e) 'Population' — the distribution of population, its concentration and the mobility of groups and individuals;

(f) 'Recreation' — the distribution of recreational facilities and the variation in recreational resources;

(g) 'Settlement' — the siting of settlements, spheres of influence and settlement functions;

(h) 'Soils and Vegetation' — vegetation, soil structure and the ecological balance of resources;

(i) 'Towns and Cities' — functional zones, hierarchies of urban settlements and the processes of urbanization;

(j) 'Transport' — spatial interaction, the 'friction of distance' and the development of transport networks;

(k) 'Weather and Climate' — the concepts related to climatic processes, and climatic gradients and types.

In the process of selection of the main themes in geography to be considered in the construction of humanities curriculum units it will be necessary to look at some frameworks for content selection. A conventional framework might be 'local/regional/national/European/world', or that of 'regional/West European/other developed world/Third World'. As geography is concerned with the location of features, functions and people, and has a major concern with causation, the variety of materials used in geography teaching is larger than in any other part of the humanities curriculum, in that quite a limited consideration of the materials for use in geographical interpretation would include maps, photographs, statistical tabulations, written accounts, audio-visual presentations of all sorts, as well as the artefacts and features of the natural and man-made environ-

Table 2: 'Ideas in Geography' (DES/HMI)

Farming

For example, technical developments may result in the reassessment of the physical environment, and possible changes in the distribution pattern of farming.

Specialization influenced by:
(a) physical environment
(b) market access
(c) tradition
(d) farm economics
(e) government intervention

Land Forms

For example, composition of rocks determines resistance to weathering.

Manufacturing

For example, industrial location factors — materials, power, labour, markets, land values, government control.

Natural Resources

For example, growth in demand increases pressure on resources — depletion, destruction, replacement.

Recreation

For example, climate affects development of recreation areas, may restrict 'season' of use.

Settlement

For example, settlements can be ordered in a hierarchy of functions, which relate to spheres of influence.

Soils and Vegetation

Towns and Cities

Transport

Weather and Climate

Population

Figure 10:   The World — National Size by value of production

Source: World Bank 1976 (generalized)

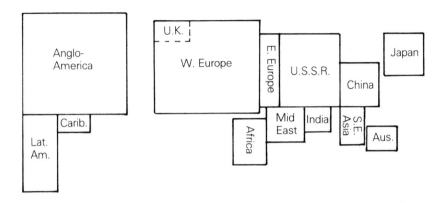

ment. It is important when considering the materials for geography that resources outside the school, as well as in other departments, are considered.

Apart from the changes in the cognitive approach to geography where we have noted the shift from topographical description to the emphasis on the explanation of patterns and processes and to the relationships between, not only man and environment, but also of communities with other communities in an environmental context, another major development has been the concern with social issues and problems, for example, with the problems of living in cities, with the conservation of environmental resources and with the problems of developing countries. The complexity of the modern world as expressed in the great variations in resource development from one part of the earth's surface to another, and the variety of perspectives developed by modern geographers, have necessitated a further development of strategies for producing insights into issues within an areal context. 'Welfare geography' can be briefly defined as being concerned with problems and issues of 'Who gets what, where?'; the subject is well described in a recent book by David M Smith *Where the Grass is Greener*. This approach seeks to probe value questions concerning human action, motivation and decision making. Geographers are seeking more sophisticated, precise evidence on which to make judgments on environmental issues, whether on the 'micro-scale' of the immediate locality, or the 'macro-scale' of the developed and underdeveloped world. Many geographers would see their discipline as intimately concerned with issues of social justice in the allocation of material and intellectual resources.

Figure 11: Northampton — a structured perception

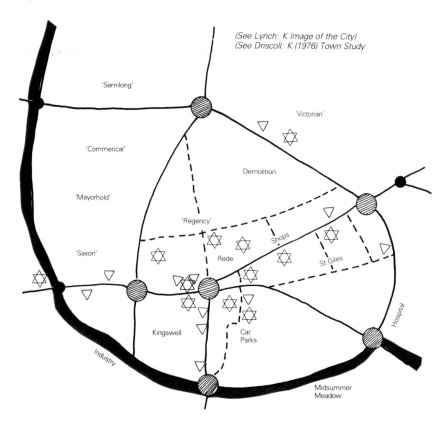

An important convention of an earlier geography, that is the geography current until perhaps the mid-1960s, was that of the 'sample study' made famous in schools by Fairgrieve and Young. The procedure was to select small communities which allegedly represented large areas of the world, by concentrating on a particular settlement or human group, as in a community concerned with some form of exploitation of the natural environment or with the processing of materials. This did not really focus on issues in the sense that modern case study material does. The sample study was essentially that of taking, for example, a coffee plantation in Brazil, a fishing port in West Scotland, or a town in Southern France and letting this stand as a representative sample for a whole regional way of life. The assumption seemed to be that somehow a body of sample studies could represent a region very often defined as a continent (outside the British Isles).

The case study, on the other hand, has a different set of assumptions. It is concerned with particular issues, often with political implications, and it uses a different framework of selection, so that whereas the sample study tended to 'select' communities to represent, usually, huge continental areas, the case study is typically concerned with people, by representing contrasts in income, or with varying lifestyles; the case study represents not so much a region, continental or national, as a particular condition or a particular geographical issue in which decisions are made. Case studies are more likely to be concerned with contrasts of population density, affluence and poverty, the level of technology, and different patterns in land resource utilization, as well as with conflicting interests in political or economic control. The emphases in much of modern geography have been of an interdisciplinary nature and this has caused some confusion in the chronic debate on whether geography is a field of study or a discipline in its own right. Geography is often seen as a combination of concepts and techniques taken from other subjects and applied to spatial relationships. Whereas history has had a relatively slow growth, in some respects, in recent times, geography has shown an enormous degree of conceptual expansion in the last two decades, so much so that the rate of expansion has caused some fundamental cleavages to appear within the subject matter and its concerns. One aspect of this is reflected in the American dichotomy of geography as an earth science and geography as a social science.

Another emphasis has been on the introduction of models or systems and the use of the data necessary to explain the processes by which these systems or models operate. Cutting across this whole field of 'real geography' has been the growth of perception studies which have emphasized those aspects of human behaviour that are seen as so important by workers in some other disciplines.[2] These aspects of study are much concerned with the way people perceive their environment, so that the map of the objective or real world is complemented by maps of the perceived world. The assumption here is that there are as many perceptions of reality as there are individual human beings involved. This has always been implicit in much geographical understanding, so that one could find travellers' tales where the European perception of the more alien environments has been in contrast to the perceptions of the indigenous inhabitants. However, the importance of perception in geography has enormously increased as a result of studies that have been made of varying images of local, and often mundane, environments. Good examples of this are the mental maps that people have of their own towns or of the rest of the countries in which they live. If one compares the mental maps that children in the north of England have of the South, with those which London children have of Scotland and the north of England, there is only a limited consonance between the two sets of perceptions.

Another aspect of the importance of perception in geography is the particular concern shown by many geographers with the spatial associations of social and economic disadvantage. In practice this learning approach encourages students to take an active role in planning and development issues, particularly in the local environment.

The proposal for a more active involvement and participation for the public in planning is well described in the government report published at the end of the 1960s called *People and Planning*, popularly known as the Skeffington Report. In this government publication the responsibilities of local government planners to encourage public participation were set down and strategies for public involvement in planning were described. However, in spite of the adjurations of central government committees to developers to consult more effectively, the last quarter of the century has witnessed a series of stark confrontations between planners and developers on the one hand and affected and disaffected members of the public on the other. One has only to recall the disputes about some of the issues listed here to be aware of the importance of a geographical understanding and interpretation in making more rational and effective judgments on these vital issues:

Coastal conservation threatened by urban leisure developments such as holiday camps and by industrial polution from oil tanker spillage.

A linked problem is the impact of motorway-generated passenger traffic on relatively unspoiled rural areas including national parks; the housing displacement may be compared with the impact of railways on Victorian cities.

Nuclear power generation and its possible side effects exemplified by the controversy surrounding Windscale and Sizewell.

Derelict industrial areas such as the decayed mining villages and towns in Durham and South Wales and the derelict docklands of the Thames and the Mersey.

Airport development and extension has been another source of bitter confrontations. The notorious examples in Britain are the proposals to create a third airport for London. There have been airport location disputes in other parts of the country

Figure 12:   Europe — 'Receding Outgroups'

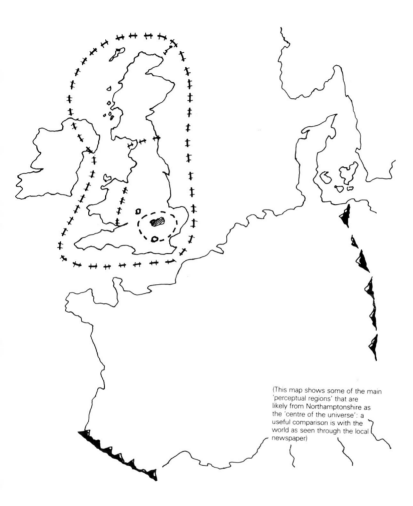

(This map shows some of the main
'perceptual regions' that are
likely from Northamptonshire as
the 'centre of the universe': a
useful comparison is with the
world as seen through the local
newspaper)

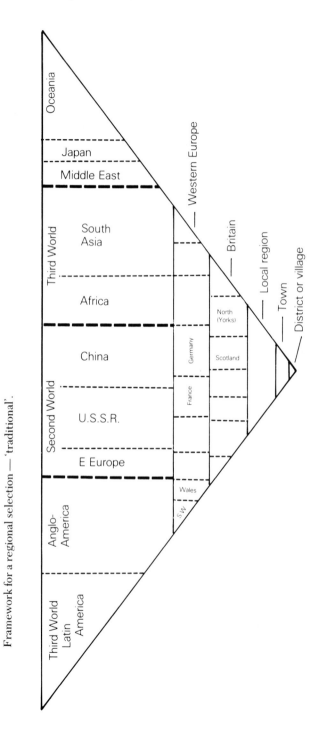

Figure 13: *Extra-terrestrial universe*

Framework for a regional selection — 'traditional'.

such as Edinburgh and this issue is likely to be a continuing source of conflict between rival interested groups.

Disparities in access to the housing market and to employment of ethnic minorities such as 'Caribbeans' and 'Asians' are likely to continue to be prominent issues in the future. Few modern texts recognize the emergence of Britain as a more ethnically heterogenous society in the last two decades, although one could claim that Britain by its very nature is a culturally heterogeneous society. Recently arrived groups, particularly from the Third World, have had more difficulty in gaining equal access and social justice than previous groups, although historians would point to the difficulties in access and acceptance of East European Jews at the turn of the twentieth century and of Catholic Irish in the middle of the nineteenth century. A recent emphasis in human geography is to go beyond the descriptive stage in explaining these issues and to encourage students to look for underlying causes, and particularly to interpret the involvement of various pressure groups in power conflicts.

All of the issues listed here have implications about the possession and exercise of economic and political power, so often the crucial questions are in the form of 'Who would lose and who would gain from this development'? and 'Why has this become an issue at this particular time'? Many of these present sharp social conflicts, as in the airport location disputes between rural conservationists and those wanting increased employment opportunities, or between those in redeveloped central urban areas wanting cheap housing and employment on the one hand and those wanting prestige hotels and offices on the other.

Issues like these illustrate the impossibility of separating human geography from political and economic issues. Similar considerations define the emergence of development studies as an important area of geographical innovation. Development studies has particular concerns with human rights and social justice. Development in the Third World[1] is closely linked with the political activities of more prosperous nations and with the economic interests of national and multinational corporations. There are close relationships between the study of economic and social development in South Asia, Africa and Latin America and the study of the character of Britain as a multi-ethnic society. Both studies are concerned with issues of social justice and with the importance of the images held by many indigenous English people of those newcomers of a different cultural background, both of those in Britain and of the peoples of 'The South'.

In all the humanities curriculum it is important that children be given a sample of the varieties of history and economics and anthropology; so it is equally important that children obtain an understanding of the variety of forms of geography. In the units some distinction has been drawn, albeit an artificial one, in that the term 'geography' in the title is used as it is related to the spatial behaviour of human beings, whereas the term 'earth science' is preferred, in this situation, to describe those elements of geography that would normally be called physical geography, or geomorphology, or geology. This is not to reinforce the division which many geographers themselves deplore, but simply to suggest that in some cases, for example, it may be easier to consider aspects of human geography as dominant, as distinct from those cases in which physical geography is of more importance.

There is a danger that the more systematic approach to geographical learning could remove one of the most enjoyable aspects of traditional geography that is the descriptive traveller's account of the natural and the man-made world. As the narrative is important in enjoying history so the descriptions that one may read in 'Splendour of Earth' or in the works of writers like Freya Stark, Eric Newby or Jan Morris are very important for the enjoyment of geography. Similarly, the work of film directors such as Akira Kurosawa, John Ford and John Schlesinger, who are endowed with a 'genius faculty' of conveying the idiosyncracies of particular places in particular eras, have a contribution to the understanding of place that cannot be equalled in other media.

If we consider those units that are listed as having 'geography' as a main label, we can see the importance of the different ideas and different aspects of geography appearing. So, for instance, if one takes A3, A9, A17 and A18, all of these are concerned with settlement geography and 'reach out' from the immediate neighbourhood of the school to changes in the regional environment. But in this, already some of the basic geographical ideas about settlement hierarchies and linkages are under consideration, as well as 'geographies' concerned with the changing natural environment and with the changing built environment. Those units with an earth science 'label' in Phase 1, such as 'The evolution and composition of the earth' and 'The earth in the solar system' are concerned with aspects of physical and mathematical geography and show traditional patterns of geographical interpretation.

Further issues related to geography will be considered in Chapters 7 and 8 which are concerned with the composition of the units.

Note

1 Many would see this as a misleading term in its suggestion of a homogeneous experience and cultural environment that simply underlies the limited prospectives held by many persons in North America and Western Europe.

2 See, for example, a useful introduction to this subject P. Gould and R. White (1974) *Mental Maps*, Penguin, and the extensive work of Brian Goodey and others on perception of the local environment.

Chapter 5

History in the Humanities Curriculum

As geography is used as a title to refer to the actuality of the surface of the earth, that which might be more appropriately entitled 'topography', but is also used to refer to the spatial analysis of the features of the earth surface and the creatures who inhabit this surface, history similarly is interpreted in two main ways which interrelate but which it is necessary to emphasize are not the same. History, on the one hand, is seen as the record of the actions of human beings in the past, but on the other hand is seen as the significant understanding of the past. It is necessary to emphasize that however much the historian may attempt to present an objective reality of what has happened in the past, in fact the conditioning influences are so strong in the perceptions of how human beings have behaved and of the relative significance of events, that this is, in practice, quite impossible.[1] So each age produces its own image of the past and hence we have historians producing, quite unconsciously, 'versions' of what happened. So English history textbooks in the nineteenth century, and through a large part of the early twentieth century, were dominated by the Whig interpretation of history, which implicitly suggested that all good human evolution was towards a form of parliamentary democracy on the British model, as it was conceived in Edwardian or late Victorian times.

This is one of the main reasons why there has been considerable suspicion about the development of concepts in history. All of us who have studied history are aware of the shadows of proto-historians, that is Marxists or Right Wing historians, who have found in history a convenient vehicle for the propagation of their own political and social beliefs; 'a useful vehicle for teaching something else'.

When we look at the problems of nationalist or racialist interpretations of history the issue presented is no less serious than that of the interpretations of Right Wing or Left Wing economists, in that older British history textbooks are suffused with negative ideas towards the non-white population of the world, and indeed towards most people born on the other side of the English Channel and the

Irish Sea. These prejudices are reflected in earlier versions of the National Anthem, which did not hesitate to interpret the behaviour of the 'others', that is the non-English, as devious and malicious. The same prejudices infuse many of the ideas which were generally current in the humanities, but history may give more evidence of this sort of prejudice than the other contributory disciplines. It may be useful here to call attention to some of the work that has been done on the examination of prejudices in history textbooks, and here one would particularly wish to cite the work by McDiarmid and Pratt, (1971) *Teaching Prejudice*, which gives a useful account of the measurement of prejudice and of some ways in which to combat it.

If the teaching of history by concepts in the broadest sense is suspect, is there then an analogy to the teaching by concepts and skills in geography? The answer certainly is 'yes', and undoubtedly, just as the topographical/regional approach in geography has prevented people coming close to the central issues that have been mentioned in the previous chapter, so the chronological approach to history beginning with 'early man' and ending very often with recent British politicians, has served little useful end, particularly as so much of this chronological approach made implicit assumptions about the special role of the British people and of the 'British destiny' to control a large part of the rest of the world. Now that this era has passed, the chronological approach, with an apparent 'end-product' of Britain shaping the destiny of a large part of the world, is less and less relevant.

What can be done is to select concepts that refer to important institutions and processes and, even more importantly, one can select crucial forms of historical experience. Appropriate concepts are taken, not necessarily from history itself, but are concepts which history shares with a number of other disciplines and fields of study. Embedded concepts are in such terms as 'monarchy', 'Parliament', 'middle class', 'trade', 'nationalism', 'communism', 'feudalism', and 'civilization'. Even then there are problems about the selection of experiences that really represent 'good educational value' rather than simply reflecting the perspectives of individual teachers, of groups of teachers, or of educationalists. In brief, the experiences selected should relate to the major features and forms of the human life cycle. For example, they might well be concerned with patterns of survival, with the conflict of ideas, beliefs and behaviour, with relationships between individuals and the institutions which have been humanly created, and with the development of skills, particularly the long story of the increasing human mastery of a great variety of technologies.

Two extremes of principle might be seen in the process of selection. Firstly, that of trying to find in history immediate relevance to the contemporary world, either a direct relevance by studying modern history or the search for analogies and comparisons with the issues that seem to be dominant at the present time. And secondly, at the other extreme, there may be the deliberate search for cross-cultural contrasts; that is the search for communities and experiences that make us question our own preconceptions. Whereas the first may have a determinist tinge in that its perspective is essentially that of the 'present time in this place', the second perspective is deliberately anti-determinist and looks towards possible worlds or possible solutions to chronic problems rather than to tried methods and interpretations.

Of similar importance are the questions concerning not only what has happened in the past and the interpretation of the past, but those related to what historians actually do. Many people who have researched in the historical field eventually conclude that the basic task of the historian is to sift evidence, draw conclusions and make provisional judgments. In a sense this is similar to the hypothetico-deductive mode of the scientist, but with an infinite number of variations and without the 'test situation'. History has the great advantage over sociology and the other social sciences of presenting a 'completed narrative' so that one can discover not only what might have happened but what actually did happen.

For children to gain an understanding of what historians do, and what their concerns are, it is necessary for them to learn to examine the evidence for particular inferences and to do this obviously the evidence they examine needs to be related to a knowledge of the context in which events happened or the personalities interacted. The use of primary sources is not distinct from the process of using secondary records, although children should certainly be led to an understanding of the difference in character between primary and secondary sources.

An example may suffice to illustrate the importance of secondary sources in providing a framework of historical knowledge. One of the important developments in the teaching of history in schools in the last few years has been the development of various forms of local history, and amongst them is the work on family history which is so well exemplified in Steel and Taylor's handbook (1973) *Family History in Schools*. Much of the work described is based on a 'three generations' theme, that is of looking at the lives of the children themselves in perspective to get an idea of timescale, then at the experiences in the lives of their parents, and then equivalent or important experiences in the lives of their grandparents. In researching into the history of their own families (and obviously here one needs to be aware of the sensitive issues relating to the 'skeletons in the cupboard' of most families), children are likely to encounter a

Figure 14:   Key Historical Ideas

MAJOR CONCERNS
(A)   Portrayal of human activity
(B)   Sequence and completion of process
(C)   Human intention in social context — 'character of age'
(D)   Evaluation of evidence — detection of bias
(E)   Identification of central issues: in past and in present
                            EVOLUTION   CONTRAST   ANALOGY
TYPICAL 'CONTENTS' RELATED TO IMPORTANT IDEAS AND
EXPERIENCES
1   LOCALITY ⎺⎺⎺THREE GENERATIONS IN A FAMILY
                      ⎽⎽⎽CHANGE IN ENVIRONMENT
2   PEOPLE IN THE PAST — selection to show contrast, similarities in terms of:
      (A)   Size of community and location
      (B)   Social and political organization
      (C)   Technology
      (D)   Belief systems
      (E)   Institutions and rituals
      All of these aspects of the study of community life are mediated by the sort of
      evidence available and its use.
3   EXPERIENCE OF 'HISTORIES', for example, Theme Dev., Era/Patch,
      Biography. Crisis and Change SIMULATIONS

variety of resource material such as photographs, newspaper cuttings
and maps of the area, written recollections of past events and places,
eye witness accounts and so on. In order to make sense of the material
that they discover and which they begin to collate, they will need
some sort of background understanding of the major issues of the
time. A good example of this would be related to the very popular
theme of 'The Home Front in the Second World War'. Here many
children may well assemble a great mass of artefact material, and indeed one of the fascinating exercises is to try to relate artefacts to local
newspaper reports and other 'documentary evidence', but the value
of the study would be enormously enhanced by an understanding of
the main pattern of events in World War II and of the restrictions and
opportunities that so affected the lives of the civilian population.

The value of the exercise is in seeing the complexity of the
process of making judgments about the past and of going through the
processes of collation to interpretation, to a possible extrapolation and
empathy and, finally, of attempting to make informed value judgments about the people and events of a past era.

One of the neglected artefacts is close at hand in many schools,
the old text book, albeit its uses are necessarily limited. Ironically this
has been forced upon many schools by the present economic string-
encies, but the use of old history text books will show the great
variation from the modern interpretations of recent history, whether
one takes, for an example, the Munich Crisis or the relative import-

Figure 15:   World History 'Experiences'

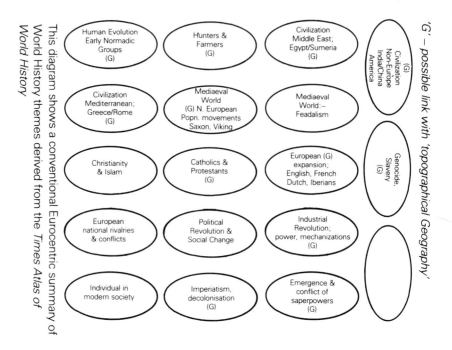

ance of the role of Britain in the Suez Crisis in the 1950s, as compared with the interpretations of the events of 'Suez' and its aftermath from the perspective of the 1970s or 1980s.

In addition to the text books there are repositories of valuable historical material in series such as *Great Newspapers Reprinted* or *The Newspapers of World War II* or, on the other hand, the series of archive units that have been produced by many local authorities dealing with recent or more remote history. Certainly the use of old school text books provides a particularly useful introduction to this basic study-skill of text book evaluation and interpretation, in that children can then be taught to see the significance of authorship in its own period of time, the audience envisaged by the author, and the way that most people, except those very special individuals who might be termed 'genius', are 'locked' into the preconceptions of the era in which they themselves lived.

Similarly 'archive' film and film-strips give great insights into the process of selection of the significant at the time. The collection of materials related to events that are likely to be 'revalued' in a relatively short time, the 'South Atlantic War of 1982', for example, is a valuable exercise for teachers and pupils to undertake.

Some comment will be made in later chapters about the importance of the teaching of study-skills, and indeed this will apply across the humanities, but the history text book and film are particularly useful for the development of analytical skills as well as for the acquisition of 'reference' skills in the use of printed and visual materials.

Can we then select the criteria for the identification of particular human experiences that have been of more 'value' than others? These are some of the factors that we would need to bear in mind when considering the process of selection.

Firstly, in history we are concerned with the portrayal of the complexity of human activity in a great variety of social and environmental contexts. History in the second sense that we referred to, is an abstract of the significant elements of human behaviour and has its focus on important issues. This is worth considering in some depth, because it is possible to see the changing emphasis in history over the last fifty years as it appears in the very often unconscious bias of the history text books, not only in a political or national sense, but also in what was selected as of historical importance. So in the earlier twentieth century, history text books tended to be dominated by political events and to be particularly suffused with the idea that the 'significant' was related to the expansionist role of the British people. In the 1930s other emphases began to appear, so instead of the 'conflict model', which had been dominant in the first quarter of the twentieth century, the 'cooperation model' began to be evident in a number of text books, particularly those whose authors were influenced by such organizations as the League of Nations Union. At the same time in the 1930s, and increasingly in the post-war period, more economic and social history was being infused into text books, so that it was not only political 'personalities' and events that were perceived as important but also social and economic developments. This was well exemplified by the great popularity of works by the Quennells *The History of Everyday Things in England* and similar texts.

It is now belatedly recognized that all these forms of history are important, so that children should have an experience of foreign international history, an experience of ancient history, an experience of early modern history, experience of contemporary social history, an experience of foreign economic history, and so on.

Secondly, historians should be shown to have a reliance on a great variety of forms of evidence, so that historians dealing with the pre-historic era where their work merges with that of the archaeologist, are concerned with, amongst other things, the application of a

Table 3:   Some Key Historical Experiences

Examples
Human survival — basic physical needs
Organization and control in small societies
Technological innovation/energy/industry — social implications
Leisure and work — changing definitions related to social forms
Homes and families — variation, interaction
Ceremonies and rituals; arts and artists
Religious systems and beliefs in their social context
Exploration and development — culture interaction, genocide
Political and social ideologies, institutions
Rural-urban relations; conflict and dependence
Population — growth, movement, decline, displacement
Communication/interaction — communities in relationship
Colonization/imperialism and their decline
Economic ideas and institutions, for example, capital and banking
Social welfare and governmental administration

People — Groups — Places — Ideas — Movements   ('Then and there',
'People in Past', 'Jackdaw type')

Conflict — cooperation   )
)
Development — regression   )   OVERARCHING
)
Individual — group   )   CONCEPTS
)
Conformity — dissent   )

← COMMUNITIES SELECTION →

variety of scientific techniques of which perhaps the most celebrated has been carbon dating of the artefacts of the past, through to the work of the contemporary historian, overwhelmed by a plethora of incidental, often ephemeral, even 'trivial' data. Historians working, for example, on the history of popular entertainment during the inter-war period in modern English history have as their problem, not that of concentrating on a very limited number of artefacts and applying analytical scientific techniques, but of sifting through an immense mass of ephemeral data, and data, moreover, that would have been seen as of little significance by most people in the time being studied.

Thirdly, it is important that children understand the uses to which history may be put by persons anxious to derive certain messages from the experiences of the past; so that a crucial learning process for children is the detection of bias and prejudice, both conscious and unconscious.

Fourthly, history reveals not only unique experiences, on the assumption that no two human experiences are indentical, but also stresses the considerable degree of commonality in human experience in certain respects; that is, forms of religious or political or social experience that may transcend the boundaries of time and of locality. Some examples of what the author of this document believes to be particularly vital experiences are the following:

(a) Family history, which can be highly personalized and which shows the complexity of the evidence on which historians work, and also which can be compared from the micro-scale of studying one's own family to the macro-scale of looking at families in other places in other times set against a background of national or international developments.

(b) Creation myths. I have suggested that many of the most important and interesting developments in the field of humanities are in the marginal areas between disciplines; myths of creation show the close relationships between history, literature and mythology. The study of myths, whether of our own civilization or of its forerunners, for example, the Graeco-Roman and Judaic worlds, shows the fundamental need of all groups of people for some form of historical perspective. It has well been said that people without a sense of history are like individuals without a memory, and here we have numerous illustrations of how people have attempted to make sense of their past, particularly in terms of the evolution of what they determine as their own 'in group' and out of the experience of the past to make sense of their present circumstances.

(c) The pre-technological era. It seems likely that many historians, when they are writing the history of the last 200 years, will see the significant change in the great political and social revolutions of the eighteenth and nineteenth centuries, but even more likely they will see the fundamental change in human experience as the consequence of the development of mechanical power. It is particularly important for children to gain some understanding of what life was like before the application of mechanical power to the answering of defined and 'manufactured' human needs, so that they can gain some idea of life as it was in the pre-technical era when, for most communities, there was no feeling that the life experience of the next generation would be markedly different from that of its predecessors. Similarly, for most people there was no awareness of the immediate community as one part of an enormously dense and complex network of communities that reached across the globe. These studies related to life in a pre-technical era will obviously have a major importance in other disciplinary studies, particularly those of geography and anthropology, but history can show what happened in actual communities as the pace and perceptions of life were changed by human mastery of the technologies of mass production.

(d)   It is important that children understand, as a development of the previous theme, life in the pre-technical society, and the changes that may be brought about by one major technological development. A good example of this would be the study of life in the early railway age, to show how the face of Britain was transformed by the application of one major invention, the steam engine, to the need for rapid, efficient transport of goods and people.

Consideration of the railway age should bring in evidence in a great variety of recorded experience, from the early art of photography, which only developed a little later than the steam railway itself, to the great outpouring of information which was characteristic of the early Victorian era, whether in statistical form or in the recording of eye witness accounts, the production of maps and in the changes related to the evaluation of the great network of railways that was developed in Britain from the 1840s through to the 1880s. This sort of study may also help to dispel some of the myths so often propagated by many of the history text books, that is for instance that the fastest growing towns in the mid-nineteenth century were the industrial towns, whereas in fact, it was their opposite in urban character, the seaside resorts, that grew most quickly during this period of time.

Again one would think that this sort of theme is by its nature cross-disciplinary in that something like the effects of the railway age cannot be conceived without a study also of the geographical and economic factors in this major change in the 'national fabric'.

(e)   Another example of a particularly significant experience, at least in the author's view, is that of internecine conflict. Not only is this sort of conflict most often concerned with fundamental value issues, but it has a particularly useful form of self-identifying empathy in that, as in any form of civil conflict, whether an industrial dispute or a civil war, it is possible for the dispute lines to cut through individual families and homes, and here also one encounters sharply contrasted perceptions of the events that took place.

Of a similar nature are the conflicts of interest present in many fast changing societies. As in geography, questions about values and sectional interests are particularly important so that essential questions are 'Who lost and who gained?' and 'Why was this issue particularly important at this time?'

Historians and sociologists have many common interests; amongst them are the reinterpretation of social relationships in the past. Dramatic examples of these reinterpretations concern the roles of policemen and soldiers particularly in relationship to working-class movement. These relationships have been examined by modern writers in plays such as *Sergeant Musgrave's Dance* and *Stocker's Copper*, which are good examples of 'drama in history'.

This is particularly useful in developing analogies and contrasts from one form of conflict to another, so that one can extend from the very local scale to the world-wide scale, and also study various forms of conflict resolution. It may be that history text books in the past have over-emphasized the 'conflict model' of historical development at the expense of the effective cooperative strategy.

(f) Some of the themes to be chosen should serve to dispel the continuing and endemic myths of national character as though this were a fixed quality that deviated little over time. Wartime propoganda is full of myths about the permanent 'savagery of the Hun', the 'perfidiousness of the British', the 'vacillating French' and so on. All the evidence shows that although we might tentatively begin to describe something as national character, at a particular time, this is far from being a fixed entity, so that travellers visiting Britain in the eighteenth century commented on the markedly extrovert and disorderly behaviour of the British, whereas a hundred years later travellers visiting England were all the time conscious of the reserved character of many of the British that they met, and of their external conformity to social and administrative pressures.

(g) There is the enormous importance of ideological or religious beliefs in human motivation; the problems of outsiders who do not conform to the pressures of a particular time and locality, issues produced by belief systems with different rationales, for example, Church v. State in the Reformation. The virulence with which a belief is held has no relation to its validity: as Nietsche observed 'A casual stroll through a lunatic asylum shows that faith does not prove anything'.

(h) The western interpretation of time is likely to be the one most appropriate for this particular form of technologically dominated society, but it is important to study societies or communities with concepts of time different from our own, for example, 'native' Australian, as it is to study North American Indian societies with different conceptions of territorial ownership. An instructive exercise in the production of time-lines on a Western base is to compare the perspectives within the chronologies of other world-cultures such as those of China or Islam. An implicit assumption in many history text-books, and not only in those published a while ago, is that peoples and places only began to exist, in a real sense, with European 'discovery'. The distortion rendered by this sort of ethnocentric perspective can be partly modified by re-interpreting the European arrival from the indigenous viewpoint. 'To see ourselves as others see us' should be applied to 'nations' or 'societies' as much as to individuals. 'Culture conflict' studies invariably show the importance of totally different perceptions of 'human-ness' by groups in confrontation, as well as differences in technology which in longer historical time may represent a very temporary superiority by one human group over another.

'Story in History'

The popularity of the story in history, both with children and adults, needs to be recognized and respected, especially as listening, whether to a live person or to the radio, may be a dying art. However the traditional form of such subject matter as that of great heroes often of 'noble descent' or 'over achievers from humble origins' needs modification by other interpretations and perspectives. The great danger of the story approach to history is that it relies too much on the histrionic and narrative descriptive skills of individual teachers and also their ability to free themselves from their own historical, social and political conceptions of the essential 'message' of the story. Amongst the most useful stories are those that counterpoise a traditional account with one from another cross-cultural or adversary position perspective.

The essential experience of 'living in the past' is more surely caught in drama[2] than in most text book history accounts in that being 'inside an individual, inside an era' requires the same sort of mental and emotional empathy as that of the 'Strasberg Method'. From this we might conclude that a better understanding may come from two or more individuals with different cultural assumptions re-interpreting the same given situation, as from a single derivative account, very often uncritically presented so that what is being given under the guise of history is in fact a multi-level mythic interpretation. A better way of understanding cross cultural contact than by reading about it, or hearing about it, is through a simulation such as Rafa Rafa[3] where two sharply different cultures meet. One group from the 'alpha culture' is 'fun loving, superstitious, honouring their elders and enjoy touching one another'. People in the opposed 'beta culture' are 'hard working, business like, foreign speaking, and do not like to be close to one another'. Out of this confrontation can come a varying number of accounts that reveal the problems of overcoming differences in surface behaviour to reach down to a common humanity.

'Oral history' has now emerged as a major development in education and as a field of popular research; the field is best approached through the works of Paul Thompson, George Evans and Ronald Blythe in England, and Studs Terkel in the USA.

Many children assimilate limited definitions of history because they fail to see history as a continuing process of change, so that logically no distinction between 'history' and the 'future' can be discerned except by reference to the evanescent present. 'The historian is a prophet looking backwards'. In curriculum terms there is an obvious 'claim' for the study of changing institutions, artefacts and ideas over a substantial period of time — the 'longitudinal reference' — as well as the inter-relationships of people, places and things in one delimited age or era — 'the lateral reference'. It is noticeable that there is an increasing emphasis by some American and European historians and social scientists on the 'Emerging Present' conceived of as 'moving line' which reflects the recent past of about a century, and 'predictive stances' towards the possible scenarios of the 'close future', perhaps the next forty or fifty years.

Further issues related to history will be discussed in chapters 7 and 8.

Note

1   A stimulating discussion is in D. Lowenthal (1985) *The Past is a Foreign Country*, CUP.
2   For an outstanding exposition of this approach see C. O'Neill and A. Lambert *Drama Structures*.
3   See the current 'Oxfam' catalogue.

Chapter 6

Social Sciences and the Humanities

In the first chapter some indication was given of the varying definitions of social sciences and humanities and it is not proposed to pursue this theme at length. In general, the social sciences and their derivative curricular form called social studies have had a 'bad press'. Social studies flourished as a school subject relatively briefly in the first part of the 1950s and then succumbed to a number of pressures. This 'bad image' in some educational quarters may need rather more contextual explanation than subjects such as history and geography, the 'curriculum validity' of which would be questioned in relatively few conventional schools. Amongst the forces that ensured its collapse in most schools which had developed it as a curriculum subject, there were two main factors.

Firstly, social studies evoked a great amount of hostility from practitioners of other established school subjects, notably history and geography teachers, but also from teachers of English. Many of these teachers saw social studies as a fashionable interloper intent on destroying the basis of the established humanities/arts curriculum; the degree of opposition evoked by proponents of social studies can be seen in the professional journals of the 1950s. Far more fundamental as the reason for its collapse was the fact that it lacked an adequate conceptual disciplinary structure, so social studies syllabuses exhibited a great degree of variation and many of them seemed to be determined on a serendipity principle, that is, any topic that was judged by the assistant teacher or often the headteacher to be of significance was taken up for a partial study. Rather like some sixth-form general studies schemes, there was no structure and coherence established over a long period of time — so much so that one could not point to a rational, coherent, integrated curriculum extending for a period of three, four or five years. Because of these characteristics, social studies relatively quickly declined to a low status compared with 'established' subjects and its passing in many schools was marked also by its downward placement in the 'bottom' streams of some secondary modern schools. In other words, it was the subject designated for those children for whom the academic curriculum had been judged a failure.

Its demise in most schools passed without sorrow or regret on the part of most secondary teachers, although it had perhaps a longer period of acceptance in a relatively small number of primary schools. In the late 1960s a revival of the social sciences as a part of the secondary curriculum began to take place.

Economics had long been established as a 'respectable' subject, particularly in the sixth-form, and during the late 1960s and the 1970s the number of people taking economics in the sixth-form and in the fifth form increased five-fold. Sociology was slower to follow and it is notable now that, although economics at 'A' level is the sixth most popular subject in England and Wales, sociology is ranked in schools at eleventh place. Notable, however, has been the marked growth in popularity of sociology and economics in further education, at 'O' level as well as at 'A' level; and undoubtedly if one looks at the projection of trends in terms of subject popularity, both economics and sociology would appear to still be rising in acceptability in the schools.

Much more hesitation has been expressed in many schools at the introduction of the social sciences below the fourth and fifth years, but a counter-movement to introduce the concepts of the social sciences rather than the subjects themselves, as distinct entities, has been evident in many secondary schools, particularly those that have developed a 'humanities curriculum', that is a form of interdisciplinary curriculum largely based in the majority of schools on history and geography. Many of these schools have found the concepts of the social science disciplines so important that, quite deliberately, concepts and knowledge from these disciplines have been introduced either as units to which subject labels could be attached or, more often, as a reinforcement and extension of basic concepts already encountered in geography, history, religious education and so on.

Undoubtedly part of the appeal of the social sciences is that the subject matter which the various social sciences disciplines choose to interpret is of major concern to the majority of secondary age children; one might generalize further and claim that it is vital to virtually all persons living in contemporary Britain. Below is a list of subjects taken from a number of Schools Council projects such as the Humanities Project, the General Studies Project and from a range of text books dealing with the social sciences in the secondary age years.

1   Family life and kinship
2   Human differences, biological and cultural
3   Home and community
4   Health and safety

Some indication has already been given of changes in the structure of the more accepted established social disciplines in schools. The form that the social sciences takes in the syllabuses that have been developed in the last ten years is essentially similar to that which has taken place in a large part of the curriculum; the approach is much more analytical and, above all, the structure of learning is determined by concepts, skills and attitudes to be acquired. These are central and determine the selection of the subject matter for study.

Sociology has perhaps the most relevance to the humanities curriculum in the secondary years, although presumably people with a strong interest in political science or economics might challenge this; but if one looks at the crucial concepts in modern sociology, which are so important for an understanding of many of the issues explored in the humanities, whether the previous subject labelling has been history, geography or religious studies, or even English, then the necessity for their inclusion can hardly be questioned.

Sociologists are divided in their basic interpretations and allegiances in much the same way that historians or geographers are. There are a number of cleavages of interests and opinion, but fundamental is that between two large groups. Traditional 'positivist' sociologists usually stress the analysis of society based as far as possible on objective data; that is they work on materials such as census material, sample surveys of opinion, various types of demographic and administrative data and from this derive their conclusions or the materials for hypothesis testing. Opposed to this are an increasingly important group who in some respects have reverted to an earlier approach closer to that of the social anthropologist. This approach is described by a number of terms, amongst them some rather obscure ones such as 'phenomenology' and 'ethnomethodology', but basically what they have in common is the great stress that is placed on the world as it is perceived by the individual, so that institutions and social relationships are seen as the combined perceptions of individuals. It is these perceptions from a variety of individuals that endow the institutions and the issues with reality, rather than the statistically objective account. This particular perspective relates to one of the current popular assumptions in education: that all knowledge is socially constructed by individuals. Although the approaches differ so sharply in terms of the more objective, statistically-orientated sociologists and the new sociologists who are concerned with individual perceptions, and one of whose methods of working is most usually described as 'participant observation', nevertheless their interests are approximately the same, so if one looks at the basic concerns of sociology, one finds such subjects as the following:-

Gender and sex
Social class
Ethnic group
Community
Cultural values
Deviant behaviour
Institutional functions
Roles and status
Bureaucracy
Customs and behaviour
Self concept
Prejudice and discrimination
Mass media
Work and leisure

and so on.

The change from the completely objective stance which was normally recognized to be one of the criteria of the approach of social scientists and its displacement, at least for some people, by that of participant observation, that is of getting inside a primary group or institution and appraising the world more or less as an insider, has of course, changed some of the emphases in the ways in which sociologists work and the ways in which their research findings are presented. To a large extent these issues are not likely to affect the teaching of sociology in schools below the sixth-form, except perhaps to bring a much needed balance, in the opinion of many, in the manner of the use of evidence. Whereas history until relatively recently tended to be non-statistical, and where the dominant form was the narrative description of an event or series of events in the past, now historians increasingly look towards quantitative data to support or refute an interpretation. In some ways the movement of sociology has been in the opposite direction. That is, sociologists who from the late nineteenth century had been dominated by the need to interpret quantitative data, and its interpolation, increasingly accept also the subjective account of the researcher inside the group or the institution as a valid form of evidence. There is obviously a difficulty at a higher education level in the consideration of the validity of the evidence and the necessity to present a variety of viewpoints on an issue; but at school level the combination of quantitative data and personal accounts should go some way to restoring a modified interpretation. Certainly the formulation of questions by sociologists has had wide-reaching effects on the research procedures, and on the questions asked, by modern historians and geographers, in that sociologists have tended to ask questions in a more methodical way, perhaps more closely related to the pattern of work associated with the Natural Sciences and have also been more rigorous, in many cases, in their analysis of data.

Whereas traditionally sociologists have tended to focus on large-scale modern societies, particularly the societies of which they themselves were a part, anthropologists have mainly been concerned with the investigation of small-scale societies, generally with a relatively undeveloped technology as compared with modern societies in Western Europe or North America.

Anthropology has three main dimensions: *cultural* symbolic anthropology, which is essentially concerned with the belief systems and artefacts of societies; *physical* anthropology, which is largely concerned with biological differences amongst human groups; and *social* anthropology, which refers to social relationships between or amongst primitive societies and also within the members of the societies, and is, of course, because of its social preoccupation, much closer in its approach, and in its working material, to sociology.

The value of studies in cultural and social anthropology in schools is that well expressed in the title of an anthropology textbook of some three decades ago. It is called *Mirror for Man* and the main objective of the author, the American anthropologist, Clyde Kluckohn, was to hold up a mirror to contemporary American society and thereby give another dimension to the understanding of humanness and, by removing some of the 'clutter' of a modern large-scale technologically and socially complex society, to analyze basic 'tribal' human behaviour. The 'early' anthropologist, particularly, has been concerned with the significance of myth and ritual in understanding much of the behaviour of small-scale human groups, with the assumption that the ritual element that accompanies so much of life has importance for all human beings and endows the practices of living with particular significance. Hence the interest of 'early' anthropologists such as Bronislaw Malinowski, Margaret Mead, Ruth Benedict, and others, in festivals and rituals, whether these accompany feasting and celebrations, or the great 'passages of life' such as birth, death and marriage, or the rituals that accompany seasonal climatic changes.

Perhaps of most value is the understanding that culture is the most important determining factor in the way in which human beings attempt to not only deal with the basic problems of survival and development, but also in marking important occasions. This is a vital factor when one looks at theories of human evolution and the diversity as well as the commonality in these theories. There is also a great diversity of interpretations about the validity of the forms of stratification, and the relationships between sub-groups. Particularly good examples of these would be the variety of roles and functions performed by men and women, so that children may grow to an understanding that the relationship in western society which has largely been one of male dominance is not a universal pattern, and that the elderly people in a primary group, as well as in larger groups, can receive veneration rather than relegation.

It is important also to see how these perceptions of social roles are closely related to the economic structures of societies. Although both sociologists and anthropologists have produced so much material of the participant-observation type, there is, nevertheless, an enormous amount of material from sociologists that helps to illuminate, as well as to explain, large-scale changes.[1]

Psychology is even more remote from the curriculum in the overwhelming majority of schools, except as it is applied consciously or unconsciously by the staff in the running of the school and by the pupils in their relationships with teachers. Nevertheless certain of the major themes that will be suggested in the chapter on curriculum units are heavily dependent on some basic ideas that are more associated with psychology than with the other social sciences. In the study of psychology there are close relationships with the study of biology, particularly in the study of the functioning of the brain and of the nervous system. Psychology shares with sociology and anthropology a concern with the factors that encourage or inhibit the mental growth of the individual and, of course, is fundamentally concerned with the formation of personality. Psychology itself provides much of the conceptual structure necessary to 'get to grips' with the chronic debate about the relative importance of genetic inheritance and environmental conditioning. The concern of psychology with such basic facets of human behaviour as motivation and interest and emotion, as well as rationality, means that it is at the core of any study of the behaviour of human beings in a social context.

The importance of psychology in history, geography and sociology has been enormously enhanced by the developments in all these disciplines that stress the importance of the perceptual world as well as of the objective world, and this importance also carries over into the related fields of linguistics, literature, and mythology. There is much evidence of the importance of the way individuals understand the world and how they 'structure' the world in accord with their perceptions. Also to be considered is the important association of this with language development. Certainly, to understand a considerable amount of the materials in the units recommended in Phase Four, that is those units concerned with studies of conflict and cooperation, it will be enormously helpful to have some understanding of the basic psychological processes as well as of the importance of the relationships between the conscious and the unconscious mind.

Most teachers would express grave doubts about the usefulness or appropriateness of a module with the label 'psychology', but would accept the usefulness of some of the basic concepts of psychology that are necessary for the understanding of human behaviour, whether as human behaviour on a micro-scale, that is of one person towards another person, or amongst a number of persons, as well as of understanding the behaviour of groups or individuals towards one another. An understanding of some basic psychology gives a considerable degree of enlightenment to case studies which are concerned with human aggression or human prejudice, in that a case study, for instance, which showed completely hostile perceptions of one group by another, or the associated developments of stereotypes by which individuals are endowed with characteristics alleged to be those of a whole group, are an essential part of understanding relationships between large groups of people, particularly where they are in situations of confrontation or conflict. Much of the material used to develop and illuminate psychological concepts seems to have an inherent fascination for many children, particularly when these ideas are developed in the form of simulations or role play exercises.

The study of politics in the school has, like psychology and sociology, been viewed with a degree of suspicion, but readers of this 'document' will be aware of how much emphasis needs to be given to the development of political literacy in young persons before they leave school, and indeed while they are still at school. The degree of political unawareness has been well illustrated by a number of research studies[2]. This degree of political unawareness or ignorance may be seen as a threat to the whole of our society, particularly when Britain is undergoing a series of fundamental social and economic changes which may not always be construed as leading to an improvement in the quality of life. It is in these situations that democratic institutions which have been established over a very long period of time may seen to be most threatened. As the other social sciences have been concerned not so much with the selection of themes on a conventional basis, but with a concentration on the conceptual structure of understanding, so the Political Education Project has been concerned with the development of knowledge, skills and attitudes that will enhance not only understanding but a desire to participate in the political process.

There are three main areas of concern in the curricular development of political education, and all of these are concerned with the development not only of knowledge and understanding but also with the ability to make informed value judgments on political processes and issues. These three areas have been defined as, firstly, understanding the machinery of the political organization process, which would extend on a micro-scale from perhaps a Parish Council, Parish Meeting or School Council, or indeed the student's own family, through to an understanding of the machinery of international negotiation. The second area is an understanding of the main controversial issues that are current in contemporary Britain and the world and which are particularly important; it is this understanding of ideological factors that has probably been the least effectively taught in the past, simply because an understanding of the ideologies of a particular party are not sufficient without the understanding of how ideologies have evolved and what the reasons for their evolution are. Thirdly, it is necessary to have an understanding of the individuals who form the interest groups in the political process. Perhaps the crucial understanding that so many students in school lack is that of the decision-making process that goes on at all levels, and the sort of factors that need to be taken into account when one attempts to understand why decisions have been made or avoided.

The central 'core' of the political education programme has been defined by three overarching concepts: that of 'government', which is concerned with power and authority; of 'relationship' which is concerned with law, justice and representation; and that of 'people', concerned with freedom, welfare and individuality. Reproduced from a handbook on *Political Education and Political Literacy* (1978) is a tabulation (table 4) summarizing the necessary conceptual structure of political education in schools, as interpreted by Professor Bernard Crick. The book from which this table is abstracted is strongly recommended as basic reading for those schools contemplating the development of political education in the humanities curriculum.

Economics has probably been seen as the most 'respectable' of the social science subjects studies in schools, and certainly its popularity shows no signs of diminution. There are really two particular claims for the consideration of the teaching of economic concepts in school. Firstly, it is certainly important for pupils likely to be studying economics in the 'secondary' fourth and fifth years to have an opportunity of understanding its subject matter and conceptual structure in the early secondary years before committing themselves to the study of it at a higher examination-orientated level.

Table 4: Conceptual Structure for the Political Education Project

TABULAR SUMMARY

Government

Power	*Force*	*Authority*	*Order*
The ability to achieve an intended effect either by force or more usually by claims to authority	Physical pressure or use of weapons to achieve an intended effect — latent in all government, constant in none	Respect and obedience given by virtue of an institution, group or person fulfilling a function agreed to be needed and in which he or it has superior knowledge or skill	When expectations are fulfilled and calculations can be made without fear of all the circumstances and assumptions changing

Relationships

Law	*Justice*	*Representation*	*Pressure*
The body of general rules made, published and enforced by governments and recognized as binding by the government even if not as just	What is due to people as the result of some process accepted as fair irrespective of the outcome	The claim for the few to represent the many because they embody some external attribute, of which popular consent is only one of many	All the means by which government and people influence each other, other than by law or by force

People

Natural rights	*Individuality*	*Freedom*	*Welfare*
The minimum conditions for proper human existence — prior even to legal and political rights	What we perceive as unique to each man and to mankind — to be distinguished from individualism, a purely nineteenth-century doctrine	The making of choices and doing things of public significance in a self-willed and uncoerced way	The belief that the prosperity and happiness of individuals and communities is a concern of government, not merely mere survival

From Crick, B and Porter, A (1978) *Political Education an l Political Literacy*

Figure 16:   Some Problems in 'Social' Disciplines

1   WHAT IS ESSENTIALLY HUMAN ABOUT HUMAN BEINGS?
2   HOW DO INDIVIDUALS DIFFER?
3   HOW DO HUMAN SOCIETIES MAKE DECISIONS?
4   HOW DO IDEAS EVOLVE IN HUMAN GROUPS?

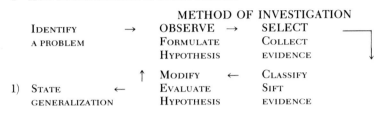

METHOD OF INVESTIGATION

IDENTIFY	→	OBSERVE →	SELECT	
A PROBLEM		FORMULATE	COLLECT	
		HYPOTHESIS	EVIDENCE	

	↑	MODIFY ←	CLASSIFY
1) STATE	←	EVALUATE	SIFT
GENERALIZATION		HYPOTHESIS	EVIDENCE

2)   *USE*

APPLICABLE SKILLS

| DISCIPLINE | TECHNICAL | FORMS OF |
| CONCEPTS | APPLICATIONS | PRESENTATION |

Secondly, and far more importantly, economic ideas underpin much of the understanding of the basic themes and issues studied by geographers and historians. There is a considerable amount of work that has been undertaken on what are the appropriate economic ideas and strategies for teaching economics in the early secondary years, the sources for which are given in the bibliography at the end of this handbook. But basically one starts with the postulate of economic studies that economics is about the allocation of scarce resources in a situation where the wants of people are virtually unlimited. Immediately one interprets economics in these terms, some of the basic issues are readily acceptable for the significance that they have. There are a number of well-tested simulation games which explain some of the basic economic processes, such as those of 'supply and demand', 'division of labour', and even of 'the money market'. Aspects of the money market are certainly well exemplified by that most popular of board games *Monopoly*. Even such an apparently daunting economic concept as that of 'diminishing marginal utility' can be relatively easily comprehended by the not-very-alert child. 'Diminishing marginal utility', for instance, is well exemplified by the consumption of any favourite confectionery and the associated diminishing value to the child of each successive particle of the sweet. A possible 'operational example' would be to give the children chocolate and then to measure the diminution of enjoyment as more and more bars of chocolate were consumed, the chocolate of course to be purchased by the children themselves.

Similar exercises in carrying out a process which may well be a

Table 5: Three 'Social' *Projects*

A   History, Geography and Social Sciences (T P and S)

1   Communication
2   Human power/authority
3   Values/beliefs
4   Conflict/consensus
5   Similarity/difference
6   Continuity/change
7   Causes and consequences

KEY CONCEPTS

B   Schools Council Integrated Studies Project *Exploration man*

1   Complexity of individual
2   Individual in group
3   Range of human activities
4   Individuals related to societies (culture)

C   'Man, a course of study' — human/other animal relationships

1   Humanness of human beings
2   How did they become human?
3   How did they develop?

'TOOLMAKER', LANGUAGE, SOCIAL ORGANIZATION, PROLONGED
CHILDHOOD, URGE TO EXPLAIN

process related to the needs of the teacher in classrooms, such as the
assembly of booklets or materials, or the processing of books, can well
be understood from the functional arguments for specialization and
division of labour. Just as many of the basic ideas about human
behaviour can be so well exemplified by the study of a small-scale
technologically simple society, (and this is the 'bedrock' of much
cultural anthropology) so many basic economic processes can be
understood by removing the 'clutter' of the complexity of modern
living. So if one looks at the way people meet their economic needs in
a 'desert island' situation and decide about the relative intensity of
use of land, labour and capital, and the way each of these basic factors
produces opportunities and constraints, then the way is open for an
understanding of the relationship of these economic factors in more
complex sophisticated societies.

Certainly the fundamental ideas in economics of production,
distribution and consumption should present no difficulty, providing
the teaching strategy is appropriate, and providing that these are
always related as far as possible to understanding at a simple level,
where the pupils can immediately become involved in direct perception and action. As the nation itself has as its central problems those
of its economic survival and development, there is no difficulty in the
selection of important issues relating to economics. Although many of

these issues are complex, the focus on simple institutions where one can see a reflection of the national problem of low productivity and associated industrial decline, can be readily understood in the study of small-scale institutions such as farms, workshops, shops, and offices.

Certainly by the time most children have reached the end of the middle years of schooling the majority of them should be able to understand such basic ideas as 'specialization increases the quantity, quality and variety of production', 'real and monetary income are not the same', and 'income is closely related to the standard of living, which in turn has a relationship to individual productivity as well as to national productivity'. Some schools may find it possible to extend the idea of simulation beyond the conventional limits and to think of the processes of production, distribution and consumption as processes related to one simulated firm, and for the students to take roles which will give them insights into, not only the processes or production and distribution, but also to matters such as public relations, advertising, and governmental control and intervention.

Further examples of the relevance and application of the social sciences will be given in chapters 7 and 8.

Notes

1   A good example would be in the Reith Lectures of A H Halsey on changes in British society, published by Oxford University Press (revised 1985).
2   See, for example, a publication of the Hansard Society *The Political Awareness of the School Leaver* by Robert Stradling.

Chapter 7

Curriculum Units

The most important learning problem to be resolved in most schools is that of the gap that appears between the process of curriculum design and the implementation of the curriculum in classroom learning. In the author's experience if there is one essential feature to be discerned in whether the classroom learning experience of most children in a school is likely to be enhanced it is whether there is practised a consistent policy and procedure of cooperative curriculum unit planning and evaluation. Teachers are notorious for their tenacity in preserving 'professional classroom autonomy', but experience and observation suggests that only by cooperation in planning, teaching and evaluating can the skills of the most able teachers be diffused as well as the performance of the less skilled or the 'newcomers' be improved. In an era in education when many teachers may expect to be redeployed or to find it to their advantage to extend their teaching roles and experiences the cooperative unit or 'modular' system of working probably offers the most effective form of necessary retraining. For the new teacher, or the less-successful teacher, cooperation mav be almost the only real chance to learn from the experience of colleagues.

Advantages of Curriculum Units

(a) Curriculum units should allow us to define more precisely limited learning objectives which we wish to achieve, in the sense that there is a finite limit on the ideas, experiences and even the resources that we may use in the specified time to be expended. This, of course, does not imply that pupils who fail to complete the unit within a given time are then simply 'taken off it'. This is something about which the school needs to make a judgment; but it does allow teachers to put a fairly precise limit on their intentions and to judge the degree to which their intentions have been realized in pupil learning. Most units described in this book would probably require about ten to fifteen hours of pupil work, including work not done under direct teacher supervision.

(b) The production of units makes relationships with resources from other sources relatively easy to define, in that it is simple to specify for a School Library Service, a Museum Service, an Authority Audio-Visual Aids Service, and so on, more limited themes than are often given in the summary of work for a more lengthy period of time. There is also a major facility in this respect in that much material already exists in unit form; so, conventionally, schools using radio and television will already find a great deal of material in prepared units of work which are usually in the form of radio or television programmes and accompanying printed material.

Many publishers, particularly those concerned with Schools Council projects, as well as with other privately sponsored projects, have produced a study-pack of material that relates to a specific unit of study. Good examples that are used in many schools would be the George Philip kits on 'Desert and Oasis' and 'Shakespeare's England', or the Longman kits on various periods of British history, environmental studies kits from Macmillans, and so on.

(c) Probably the most important advantage is that the production of a curriculum in modular form enormously facilitates not only the identification of common objectives amongst schools but allows them also to effectively collaborate both in the cooperative planning of units, as well as in sharing resources, ideas and teaching expertise. There are some smaller schools which lack teachers with a range of experience in one of the major contributory disciplines; many, for example, do not have teachers with any training or experience in the teaching of sociology or economics.

The sharing of unit production within schools and amongst schools will not remove these problems but will do something towards the alleviation of the problem of appropriate resources provision and perhaps also of teaching strategies.

(d) Modules incorporating a defined collation of materials, with their associated ideas and learning strategies, are much easier to alter in the sequence in which they are used; they are relatively easier to replace than a whole scheme of work, and also relatively easy to change by the modification of detailed elements within the units. So in changing the emphasis in a year's or term's study, it is far easier to have a

Figure 17:   Resources for a Curriculum Unit

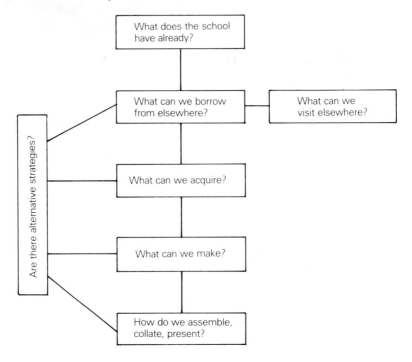

unit system than to have a continuous scheme of work where the major elements are less easily distinguished. Some people may find it significant, or perhaps ominous, that this provision of learning modules closely parallels some of the more important developments in industrial production.

(e)   Those persons who have read the foregoing chapters carefully will understand the commitment in this book to the Brunerian concept of spiral learning, in that concepts and experiences are seen as being made progressively more complex and demanding on the pupil through each of the four phases. Units make it easier to define the stages of conceptual learning achieved by the pupil and certainly make it much easier to identify the necessary prior learning as well as the necessary subsequent learning that need to be related to the study of any particular unit.

(f)   Units can provide more easily for special assessment needs. For example, it is not practical to think of one mode of assessment or even a limited number of modes of assessment that would satisfy the cognitive 'demands' of the themes presented here. The techniques that one needs to use in assessing whether the pupils have derived an initiation into systems and processes, perhaps by the use of simulation, or have acquired a degree of graphicacy by the use of maps, or of research skills in the use of historical documents, or techniques of local study for environmental work, are all dependent on the display of different skills and ideas. In each unit, where one identifies a skill to be applied or an idea to be learned, one can adjust the assessment procedure according to that need. This also relates, of course, to the way in which records of pupil progress are kept. Again it is feasible to devise an assessment schedule for each aspect of the skills and ideas presented in a unit more readily than by assessing over a term's work or over the work of a single lesson.

(g) Curriculum units can be well adapted for special needs. For example:

(i) Slow learners — the concepts can be simplified or presented in a different form. The vocabulary in the material used can be adapted for the use of slow learners and generally more thought can be given to the particular presentation or learning needs of this group of children.

(ii) The needs of the fast learners are dealt with more fully in some notes about extension studies that will be found later in the book, but basically the assumption is made that gifted children need depth and breadth in concept enrichment rather than a need to move on to material that the majority of the children will encounter later on during the 'scheme'. So, for example, rather than suggesting that the more able children work on 'the next' unit, the assumption made here is that each unit answers the conceptual learning needs of children at all levels. Whereas the slow learning children will have a more concise adapted version, the fast learning children will be presented with learning that enlarges the concept, gives them more difficult material to work on, and extends the ideas and experiences embedded in the main conceptual structure.

(h) For pupil needs the units have the advantage of being easily defined in time within the pattern of a year's work or indeed of five or six years' work. One of the great defects of the curriculum pattern in many schools, well evident in the humanities, is the 'mystery tour' element in much of the content and, indeed, in the conceptual structure. The main themes of work can be easily defined for children in

Figure 18: Algorithm for Unit Resources

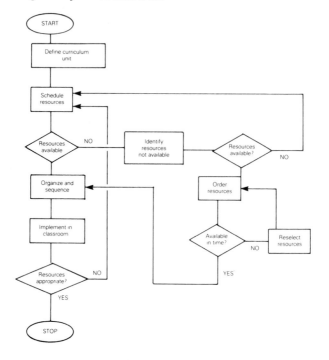

advance, which in a large proportion of cases should ensure more effective parental understanding and parental co-operation, by creating a climate of expectation about what is to be studied, and also by reinforcing material already learned. The teacher can return to the ideas developed in an earlier unit at a later date. The setting out of a programme in this easily definable form should go some way to improving the information and understanding of the curriculum for slow learners, for later arrivals in the school, for children who are absent for long periods of time, and so on.

(i)   Storage, classification and cross-reference indexing is made immensely easier if one thinks of the way a unit-based curriculum actually works. More consideration is given to the resources aspect of the curriculum unit in the chapter on that subject, but if one holds the mental image of a fairly large cardboard box in mind (although this would not be the reality of the situation, it perhaps is a useful metaphor to use when thinking of what a unit will contain and what its function will be) this 'box' would perform the following functions:

(i)   It would contain the software material that would be

used in the school, that is books, stationery, cassettes, slides, charts; it would specifically identify all this sort of resource material held within the school.

(ii) It would specify the hardware, equipment and accommodation needed, particularly where this was related to some particular timing that involved the use of specialist accommodation or the use of equipment that had to be obtained from sources outside the school.

(iii) It would specify the resources not normally held by the school itself, but would be needed to make the unit effective, for example, resources to be hired or acquired such as extra books, visual aids and, perhaps, special speakers, and also it would specify those resources that are part of the environment itself, so it would indicate places to be visited. Here would be the specifications of a fieldwork component, museums to be visited, buildings to be investigated, and so on.

Characteristics of the Curriculum Units Suggested for Consideration

Units are presented in four phases, that is for broadly the years 8–14,[1] on the assumption that some of the themes defined by the units will be tackled in the junior school, and quite a number in Phase Four will be more effectively tackled in the upper secondary school, but the majority of them I would regard as suitable for the study of pupils in the secondary years. The number of units selected for study in each year would be determined by a number of factors, the most important of which is obviously the time available for the humanities curriculum. This time needs to be assessed as (i) operational time with teacher/pupil contact; (ii) private study time, perhaps planned as a separate entity in some schools; and (iii) the time allocated for homework in the humanities.

Time allocation at the minimum end of the scale varies from about three hours, or 15 per cent or the working week, to over five hours, that is 25 per cent of the curricular contact week depending on the 'subjects' subsumed in humanities. If one assumed a working year of thirty-eight weeks, but perhaps in real terms a 'curriculum' year that is close to thirty-six weeks, then presumably the time allocated to humanities would vary from about 110 hours to 150 hours in a year of curriculum contact time. To this one would need to add homework time, in most schools, for most pupils. An average amount of time to be spent on humanities homework seems to be between two and three hours in a week. If one 'averages' across the units there would be a great variation in the amount of time that would be needed to be spent on a unit according not only to the elements that are defined within the unit theme but the ability of the children and the resources used. One would assume an average of ten hours' curriculum contact time for a unit, plus perhaps six hours of homework if the unit is contained within the humanities. Obviously much more time would be needed for units where there is an interdisciplinary focus, and there are a considerable number of these that are suggested. These units, for example, might relate to English, particularly where there is a study of literature or mythology; to science, particularly where this relates to the study of the evolution and composition of the earth or to certain biology related environmental work; to mathematics, where there is a considerable amount of geography and economics; and to design, where there is a related study of art forms.

Unit Construction

One possible format for the construction of a unit would be to have the following classificatory system:

Unit Title

1 *Statement of main ideas, and skills and experiences, that the pupils should learn or encounter*
  This statement should relate closely to the learning objectives of the curriculum unit, whether in the form of ideas and experiences or in the acquisition of the necessary skills to make the learning effective.
2 *Links with other units in the humanities curriculum*
  This would need to specify not only the content but the ideas being established or developed and the use of common or related skills and resources.
3 *Cross-disciplinary links*
  This would need to specify relationships with other main curricular areas, which would influence not only the resources needed but also the sequencing of units.
4 *A possible resource classification is:*
  (a) printed materials
  (b) non-book materials
  (c) external resources
5 *Extension studies*
  Extension studies would be essentially sub-units of work which would meet the needs of the more gifted children, as

well as of slower learning children. The needs of gifted children would particularly relate to the extension of concepts by provision of more complex material or more complex problems to be tackled from existing material. They would also be a form of extension, as so many of the units have a community focus, in the study of other communities in space and time, in order to make cross-cultural comparisons, and also to involve as far as possible some element of creative lateral thinking which, as I have suggested, is absent in so much of the published humanities material. The needs of slower learning children need to be considered by provision for conceptual reinforcement, by particular attention to language needs and structural simplification.

6   *Teaching and learning strategies*
This section of unit design would be particularly concerned with learning skills that are initiated or require a major development in the particular unit, as well as those that relate to special resources, such as maps, audio-visual forms, fieldwork practice and others. In many units it would be important to specify the further development of skills acquired at a lower level in units already encountered.

7   *Assessment and evaluation*
Assessment would have a common pattern which one could describe for every unit, and this would be concerned with matters such as written and oral work, presentation, initiative, and so on, as well as the assessment devices which related to the 'special feature' of units; these questions will be dealt with at greater length in the chapter on assessment. Course evaluation would probably take the form of an appraisal by the teachers involved in the use of the unit, in consideration of how effective the unit was in the overall pattern of the scheme of work and what necessary amendments would need to be made.

A few examples of planned units are given; users of this handbook are urged to plan a variety of modules before implementation of the 'scheme of work'. From Phase One is taken *Unit A7*, that is the unit *Early man and basic survival needs*. This unit obviously relates to a considerable number of disciplines, dominant amongst them anthropology, history and, to a certain extent, geography. Here are listed some of the major concepts that could be encountered; it would be necessary to take great care in selecting the units most appropriate for individual groups of children, as well as the ideas to be developed.

Virtually all these concepts would be equally applicable in other study units, conspicuously A13, but I use the term 'encountered' in the sense of not thoroughly understanding a concept at this stage of study, but as acquiring an elementary understanding of the concept, which will be enriched later on in the course.

1 (i) Some of the important concepts are the following:-

    (a) Early human societies were very small in scale and very vulnerable to natural hazards.

    (b) Survival was dependent on adapting simple technologies in the provision of food, shelter, mobility, to immediate needs.

    (c) Even the most primitive societies appear to have had some division of labour in order to develop special skills, and hence make survival more likely.

    (d) Environmental factors were enormously powerful in affecting all aspects of life.

    (e) Belief systems were commonly shared by all individuals in the community and were invariably related to natural phenomena.

    (f) There were very close relationships between the limited technology that these societies possessed, their art forms and their religious beliefs, and these beliefs were strongly enforced by ritual and custom.

    (g) These societies had very limited perceptions of the world and of life and very restricted cultural interpretations.

    (h) In general one would support the 'Darwinian' thesis about the survival of the fittest and the survival of those societies most readily adaptable to changing environmental challenge.

    (i) Social organization was determined by the functions of the individual in the group and in these functions age and sex had a major importance.

    (j) One of the important features of survival was the effectiveness of the learned language and communication system and how readily it answered the cognitive and affective needs of the group.

    (k) Survival was very dependent on cooperation amongst all the members of the group.

    (l) The extended family seems to be much more important in most primitive communities than the nuclear family, so there is not a uniquely close emotional tie between 'biological' parents and their children.

(m) Social and technicl change came as a response to an external stimulus or more often by adaptation from the ideas and technologies of other societies.

(ii) Special skills necessary for this unit — relate to learning strategies.

2 *Links with other units in the humanities curriculum*
The most important links are obviously all of those that deal with societies with a relatively simple technology, whether past or present, or with simulated types of societies such as those worked on in the 'desert island' theme. The units that most closely relate to this unit conceptually are A4, A8, A10, A12, B9, B12, B13, B20, B21, C7 and D8.

3 *Cross-disciplinary links*
The closest links are obviously with science; in human biology, especially growth and development as it is manifested in childhood. There are links with English in the study of the basics of language construction and communication skills. There would be enormous scope for drama in this study particularly with dramatic adaptations of the ideas of novelists such as William Golding, as well as group drama, which encourages empathy and analysis.

4 *Resources*
The classification here is probably an over-simple one, but it will give an idea of the sort of resource schedule that is appropriate.

More detailed information about resources will obviously have to await the time when a group of teachers can undertake the exercise of scheduling all the resources needed.

(a) (i) Textbooks

(ii) Reference books held by the school and those externally required, for example, from a Schools Library Service.

(iii) Work sheets produced by the school or by a consortium of schools.

(b) (i) Television and video-recording — examples of useful programmes would be those current and recent series provided for schools by BBC and the IBA companies as well as many 'adult' programmes.

(ii) Radio — the very successful series of programmes with the title *Man* and the accompanying literature would be invaluable.

(iii) Film (increasingly available on video) — there are a considerable number of films on primitive societies and some of these are concerned with what archaeologists and historians have recently discovered by the application of advanced scientific techniques.

    (iv)   Simulation stimulus materials, sound and visual.

(c)   External:

    (i)   Museums, for example, and especially, the British Museum, the Science Museum and the Natural History Museum.

    (ii)   A local 'wild-scape'.

5 *Extension studies*

(a)   A comparison of paleolithic, neolithic and Bronze Age societies with more technologically advanced societies.

(b)   An imaginary exercise using a simulation: there are a number of these available in published form which encourage lateral approaches to the 'situation'.

(c)   An empathic exercise involving a meeting between a primitive tribe in the past and a technologically advanced group.

6 *Teaching and learning strategies*

This would relate to resources and to assessment. Here I would strongly suggest that consideration be given to one of the number of excellent games or simulations concerned with primitive societies such as 'The Hunting Game' and 'Early Man'.

7 *Assessment and evaluation*

This unit would require common criteria of assessment such as written, oral and pictorial work as well as the factors of presentation and initiative, but there might be special assessment features in the use of imaginative simulations based on the life of primitive societies.

A second example — B8 'Settlement hierarchies'

1 (i) (a)   There are a variety of reasons for the location and growth of human settlements; amongst the more important would be the accessibility to natural resources, the development of commerce, manufacturing, administration, residence.

      (b)   Natural sites have considerable importance in the original location of most settlements.

      (c)   A major factor in settlement development is the accessibility of a relatively large area to the 'node'.

      (d)   There is a strong correlation between settlement

size and the number of functions provided by the settlement. These functions are usually related to the social characteristics and technological levels of the user population.

(e) Movements between settlements are usually proportional to the size of the settlements.

(f) Settlements have spheres of influence related to their population size and the nature and range of the functions they provide.

(g) Settlements grow, decline and change. An interesting example of change would be the development of settlements, based on a primary industry such as fishing or mining, towards dependence on tourism or modern manufacturing.

(h) Large-scale settlement patterns show strong cultural influences in their determination for example, whether a farming region shows a pattern of dispersed farms or relatively large uncleated villages.

(ii) Special skills are necessary for this unit, such as map-reading, use of statistics and directories, cartographic presentation.

2 The links are obviously with all units where settlement studies form a major component in the work. Links with particular units are with A6, A9, A18, B3, B6, B15, C1, C3, C10, C11 and C16.

3 There are particularly strong links with mathematics in the conceptual understanding of ratios, network-geometry, and graphic presentation. Good examples of this sort of analytical geography are given in many recently published text books.

4 *Resources*

(a) Under this heading would be considered not only the usual variety of textbooks and reference books, but also rather more specific material such as census statistics and other quantitative information, reference books, telephone directories (particularly the Yellow Pages) and specially designed worksheets.

(b) Particular use would need to be made of some of the many useful television series.

(c) Considerable reliance would be placed not only on pupil knowledge of the region, but also on fieldwork.

5 *Extension studies*

(a) A study of other settlement hierarchies, for example, the American Mid-West, the Russian Steppeland, or the Australian Outback.

(b) A study of the changing criteria of functional importance in settlements, for example, an earlier measure of functional importance was the presence of the cinema in the small town whereas an equivalent indicator for the 1980s might be the Chinese restaurant.

6   *Teaching strategies*
This would be a unit that would depend heavily on a combined and coordinated use of a variety of evidential material, particularly the coordinated use of maps, aerial photographs, statistical information, directories, bus and rail timetables, and so on. There is a necessary mixture of official printed material and printed ephemera. There are many examples in modern geography textbooks of simulation games related to the study of settlement hierarchies.

7   *Assessment and evaluation*
The especially important styles of assessment would, for the most part, depend on analysis of the data used and the effectiveness of the presentation of imaginary landscapes in a state of change. Evaluation would be related in this, as in all the other units, to its total scheme of work. Some of the criteria would question its placement in sequence with the other units, and the diagnosis of the particular prior learning which would need to be achieved before children could successfully embark on the conceptual learning developed in this particular unit.

A third example — C19 'Introduction to money'

Although there are a number of units where economic principles and ideas are involved, this is one of the few to which one could give a label that was 'economics' rather than that of any other subject.

1   *Concepts*
Money:
(a)   Money is a medium of exchange and reflects the division of labour.
(b)   Money is a measure of value against goods and services.
(c)   Money has an accountability and a saving/conservation function.
(d)   Price is a function of the quantity of money related to the volume of goods and services.
(e)   Money possesses certain characteristics; in the vast majority of cases it can be divided into sub-units and has high qualities of durability and portability.
(f)   Money may either have intrinsic value, for example, in

the form of precious metals, or it can have a value that depends on its 'status sponsorship'.

(g) The form of money is culturally determined by social values and the scarcity of resources.

2 Particular links are in the study of the idea, that money and the production and distribution of goods are related, in units A13, A18, B3, B12, B20, C13, C21, D4, D20.

3 *Cross-disciplinary links*

The main cross-disciplinary link in this unit is with Mathematics; the understanding of money systems, accounting procedures and possibly some elementary ideas of the basis of inflation.

(to be completed by the 'handbook user')

4 *Resources*

(a)

(b)

(c)

5 *Extension studies*

6 *Teaching and learning strategies*

7 *Assessment and evaluation*

Note

1 The rapid adoption of 'Integrated Humanities' in the 'common core curriculum' of the secondary fourth and fifth years in many schools suggests that planning in this modular form is appropriate to the age of 16 and beyond.

Chapter 8

Curriculum Unit Themes

Before examining the units that are suggested, it is most important that people bear in mind the warnings and adumbrations about the units I have given elsewhere in this document.

Firstly, although I have selected four phases, this represents the work that I would envisage being done in a period of at least six school years, and possibly more, dependent on the curriculum in the fourth and fifth years of secondary school which conventionally leads to external examinations.

Secondly, the units are displayed as they are related to particular phases; this is much a matter of personal 'prejudice' and there is no sacrosanct placement of any unit so it would be quite feasible, and indeed quite an interesting curriculum exercise, to print out the titles of these units on cards and rearrange them in quite a different order from the one I have suggested. This would be entirely valid. There are obviously some units that one would tend to see as more suitable for younger pupils, such as those concerned with the application of 'low level' ideas in the local community, and others that one would essentially associate with the work of 13–16 year olds in analyzing some of the complexities of the modern world. Nevertheless, there would be considerable scope for 'moving the units about'.

Thirdly, no school could possibly consider doing more than a fraction of the units outlined in the necessary depth, but the units shown here are those from which teachers, preferably cooperatively, could make a selection. This is one of the reasons why I have in phases three and four suggested many units with the same sort of 'conceptual key'; for example in phase three there are a number of units with predominant concerns in industrialization and urbanization, and in phase four a considerable number of the units are concerned with conflict and co-operation as well as with that interesting stage where the present meets the future.

Fourthly, the large number of units that I have provided reflects not only the work that I have observed in middle schools and secondary schools, but also I hope would provide some of the appropriate themes for extension studies which are so much needed for the full expression of the talents of fast learning children.

Fifthly (a final caveat) some of the titles of the units and the conceptual learning that they may imply may seem very daunting, particularly to people who have not viewed the humanities in this particular way. I think that this is not so much a matter of greater conceptual difficulty in many cases, but may simply be the use of what has become a common terminology inside developing disciplines, and this terminology has not been reflected in everyday discourse nor in much of the published advice on humanities curriculum development.

This chapter is really a continuation of chapter 7 as it is concerned with some of the main ideas that are tackled in each phase of the overall curriculum theme and some indication of the way these relate to the units; this chapter is also an introduction to a 'do-it-yourself' exercise.

The whole system of units depends on a linkage through the phases by developing ideas, attitudes, and knowledge from one phase to another. Many of the central concepts and experiences are developed in a considerable number of units and this should facilitate coherence and coordination in the overall scheme as well as within each year.

Phase One (see figure 19)

The early units in this Phase are concerned with the use of disciplines to develop identification and understanding of the self and of the local environment in the past and in the present. Some of the fundamental ideas introduce the children to the concept of 'humanities' and to its concerns. The most fundamental ideas that I have been concerned with in suggesting these units are the following:

1 The essentially human characteristics of human beings; this is the reason for much of the concentration on the study of technologically simple societies in the sense that one removes the 'clutter' of advanced complex large-scale societies.

2 The idea of the bases of individual and group differences, whether these are in physical, mental or functional differences, as these are expressed in the study of local communities and of primitive communities remote in space and time.

3 Ideas related to change and decision-making in human groups. Again these are explored largely through the study of primitive communities and of the local community.

4 Human explanations of fundamental life experiences; these go some way to develop the understanding of what mythology and folklore elements like 'fairy stories' are about.

Figure 19:   Phase One   A

1
Pre-disciplinary
Individual and
school

2
Pre-disciplinary
School and
community – enquiry
methods introduced

3
Geography
Investigating the
neighbourhood –
introduction to maps

4
*Religious studies/
anthropology*
Local beliefs and
superstitions

5
History
Family history –
three generations
'close evidence'

6
History/geography
Growth of the town
and suburb

7
*History/geography/
anthropology*
Early man and basic
survival needs

8
History/literature
Myths of Ancient
World

9
Geography
Town and suburb:
zones, houses,
interaction

10
Earth science
Evolution and
composition of the
earth

11
Earth science
The earth in solar
system – seasons,
day/night

12
*History/literature/
anthropology/
religious studies*
Creation myths,
especially non-
European cultures

13
*Geography/
anthropology*
Contemporary
technically 'primitive'
societies, for
example, Tasaday,
Amerindians,
Bushmen

14
Biology/sociology
Animal societies and
their organization, for
example, insects,
primates

15
History/geography
Early societies –
nomads and
cultivators, for
example: Sumeria
and Egypt

16
*History/
archaeology*
Introduction to
archaeology, for
example, local site,
Iron Age fort

17
Geography
Local area in its
regional context –
hierarchies and
linkages

18
Geography
Local area in change,
new towns, transport,
shops, leisure

5 The context of human life; this is where there is a strong element of earth science and is concerned with those units which introduce children to the structure of the solar system and the composition of the earth. Many of these themes are obviously shared with the science curriculum.

In addition to these ideas, subsuming many of the unit concepts are very fundamental issues such as the sources and validity of knowledge and information; some of the units deliberately force attention on a variety of sources and information such as those from archaeology, from the study of family history and from the study of local environment, for example, the traditional debates concerning the diverse accounts of the evolution of the earth and the human race that were given by traditional science and religion. It is hoped that here some ideas can be developed about the different functions and forms taken by different disciplines.

The conceptual analysis for each of the units needs to be worked out, but most of the units should show some relationship to the above mentioned ideas.

Phase Two (see figure 20)

The basic concepts and experiences of Phase One are continued and expanded.

1 Many of these studies are concerned with 'roots' in the sense of developing ideas related to social evolution and what the modern interpretation of this is, as well as with the mythology of evolution; hence there are a number of units concerned with the study of societies in the ancient world and in early Britain.

2 There are implied 'notes towards a definition of civilization' and this again explains the emphasis not only on the study of civilizations in the ancient world, but also on the varying interpretations of civilization that should come out of the studies of European expansion and discovery.

3 Patterns in human spatial relationships. These relationships are explored in the studies of village communities and farming systems.

4 The experience of life before the development of advanced technology. Again this is a continuation of some of the ideas that should have developed in Phase One about what is essentially human about human beings.

5 An introduction to the basic processes of resource produc-

Figure 20: Phase Two   B

Ancient history/ geography 1 Early Ancient World — East Mediterranean	*Ancient history/ mythology* 2 Greek city state and its evolution	*Geography/ sociology* 3 Village survey — functions and institutions	*Geography/ sociology/history* 4 Village life and work in present and past: introduction to farming decisions	*History* 5 Village and town life in early twentieth century: evidence and sources
History 6 Pre-technical era. Celtic village and Romano-British town. Family studies	*Ancient history* 7 Roman civilization. Imperial and military expansion. Social contrasts in Empire	*Geography* 8 Settlement/local area hierarchy, for example, in North America, Mid-West, Russia. Connectivity patterns	*Geography* 9 Decision-making in farming. Climate, soil vegetation factors. Case studies	*History/geography* 10 Invasion and succession in pre-technical era, for example, Saxons and Vikings, English and Normans
Geography 11 Natural resource and primary industry. Forestry and fishing. Case studies	*Politics/economics* 12 Island theme: political organization and scarce resources	*Geography/earth science* 13 Island theme. Location, climate, vegetation. Natural disasters	*Geography* 14 Farming systems — pastoral. Case studies, for example, Texas, Australia	*History* 15 Pre-technical era — travel and exploration, for example, Vikings, Maoris, Arabs

History/geography 20
Pre-technical era. European 'discovery' of world. Cross-culture contact

Ancient history/ art/religious studies/geography 5
Non-Western civilizations, for example, Central and South America

Earth science 19
Hydrosphere and its systems, for example, water cycle, weather patterns

Ancient history/ art/religious studies/geography 4
Non-Western civilizations, for example, India, China, Japan, Benin

History/geography 18
Pre-technical early modern, for example, Elizabethan village and town

Earth science 3
Landscape forms and vegetation, for example, lowland cf highland area

History/religious studies 17
Pre-technical era. Institutions, for example, mediaeval monastery, castle, gild, crusade

History/religious studies 22
Conflict in religious ideologies, for example, Islam and Christianity

Earth science/ geography 2
River systems, for example, local river cf world river-systems

Geography 16
Farming systems — tropical plantation and subsistence, for example, India, West Africa, Latin America

Geography/earth science 21
Cold regions; case studies in variations, for example, continental cf oceanic

History 1
Early technical era: migration and settlement, for example, Europeans in Americas, Australasia, Slave trade

Figure 21: Phase Three

C

97

Figure: 21 Phase Three   C (Continued)

6 *Earth science/geography*
Coastline and shore — ecological studies

7 *Geography/earth science*
Tropical regions — case studies in variations, for example, Amazonia of Sahara

8 *Earth science*
Introducing geology — composition of rocks and minerals

9 *Geography*
Natural resource and primary industry. Mining/quarrying, for example, fossil fuels, metal ores

10 *History/geography*
Pre-technical early modern. Transport systems, for example, roads, rivers, canals

11 *History/geography*
Settlement studies in pre-technical towns, for example, county/cathedral cities

12 *History/geography*
Early mechanization — Industrial Revolution; power from water and coal

13 *Geography/history*
Transport systems — trade routes. World commodities — past of present. 'Develo-port'

14 *History/geography*
Industrial location factors in early technical era in North and Central England

15 *History/geography*
'Railway age' technology and social effects. Industrial towns and seaside resorts

16 *Geography*
Settlements and interaction. Motorways and airports — location, conservation

17 *Geography/history*
Changing leisure patterns. Locality of popular holiday areas

18 *Geography/history*
Development of holiday industry, for example, English of foreign holidays

19 *Economics*
Money systems, for example, introduction to banking, insurance

20 *Geography/economics*
Manufacturing industry case studies — location factors

21 *Geography/economics*
Service industry case studies — shops, offices, location factors

22 *Geography/earth science*
Temperate regions — case studies in variation, for example, coastal maritime of

23 *Sociology/economics*
Case studies in safety, health and welfare — past and present

24 *Geography/history/economics*
'Conflict zone', for example, Middle East, South-East Asia, Central America

tion; hence the importance of the study of farming and fishing communities.

6 An introduction to the complexity of social change and economic decisions; most of these studies have a particular focus on small scale institutions.

Phase Three (see figure 21)

The basic concepts and experiences of Phase One and Phase Two are continued and developed. The following ideas are especially important:

1 The ideas concerning the patterns of complex relationships, especially those which have resulted from the development of advanced technology, which have modified the environment, and have interacted with natural processes. This group of ideas explains the importance given to the study of the landscape, the exploitation of natural resources, and to the aggregation of human populations in the processes that we call 'urbanization'.

2 The application of advanced mechanical technology to answer and expand human problems and needs; here the units are concerned with some of the more subtle ideas of human interaction, that is of the demand which is identified by human beings and which is turn serves to create further demands. Ideas are developed about the expansion of 'wants', such as 'leisure' and 'luxury goods' and their transformation into 'needs'.

3 The credits and the debits of technological development. Some of the studies here are concerned with the problems of safety, health and welfare in the modern world and with the social effects of the Industrial Revolution.

4 Experiences related to the diversity of human natural environments and the changes that they have experienced, with a particular concentration on the effect of advanced technology in making large scale changes in the natural environment. This is one of the reasons for the study of major natural regions.

5 The diversity of complex societies. These units might well be conceived as extension studies except in schools which give a particular emphasis to the humanities. These units are concerned largely with the study of non-European civilizations.

Figure 22:   Development of Models/Simulations

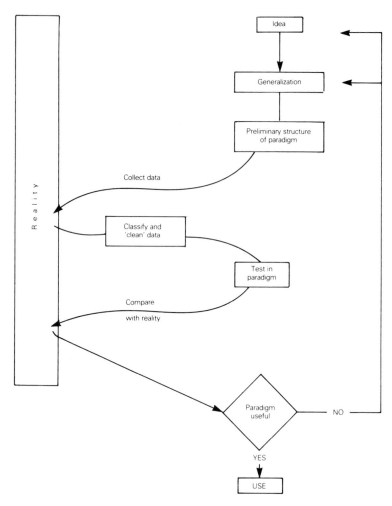

Phase Four (see figure 23)

The basic concepts and experiences introduced and developed in Phases One, Two and Three are continued and expanded. Problems and features of the modern world are dominant in this phase and some readers may think that many of the units of study are more appropriately encountered in the upper secondary years. The increasing complexity of the issues studied means an enhanced use of two particular learning techniques. One is of the 'case study', which is explained in an earlier chapter as an exemplar of the real world, on the assumption that all the issues cannot be studied but insight is most effectively gained by using a case study which usually deals with a small community rather than with a mass society. The other

Figure 23: Phase Four D

History/geography 1 Settlement studies — urban growth in early technical era, for example, Northampton, Leicester, in nineteenth century	*Geography/history* 2 Settlement studies — urbanization CS in Europe, North America, ancient world	*Geography/history* 3 Settlement studies: CS in developing world — Asia, Africa, Latin America	*Economics* 4 Simulation of land use competition and financial investment ('Monopoly')	*Geography/futurology* 5 Planning a new town. CS, for example, Milton Keynes cf Brazilia
Geography/history/economics 6 Development studies — rapid modernization, for example, Japan or Portugal of local area	*Conflict/cooperative studies* 7 Internecine conflict, for example, Civil War — seventeenth century England, Ireland in 1970s, Spain in 1930s	*Conflict/cooperative studies* 8 genocide/resolution, for example, Nazi Germany, South Africa, American West	*Conflict/cooperative studies* 9 Imperialism and national independence. CS, for example, American colonies, West Africa, Central Africa, Vietnam	*Conflict/cooperative studies* 10 Ideological/personal case studies — race, class, occupation, sex, for example, female suffrage, Great Strike, 'Black Power'
Conflict/cooperative 11 CS of individuals vs powerful institutions, for example, religious martyrs, political radicals	*Conflict/cooperative* 12 Studies relative to global scale, for example, CS of Superpowers	*Conflict/cooperative studies* 13 Law and order CS, for example, crime in cultural context. Locality vs —	*Conflict/cooperative studies* 14 Competing systems: religious institutions vs the state, for example, Reformation	*Conflict/cooperative studies* 15 Political revolution, for example, France, Russia, China

History 16
Settlement studies in developed technical era, for example, CS in nineteenth and early twentieth century

Conflict/ cooperative studies 17
Continental conflict, for example, World Wars, Napoleonic Wars

Geography/history 18
European industry — growth and change. Case studies, for example, Ruhr, Rhone

Geography/history 19
European inequalities, for example, North and South Britain, North and South Italy rural/ urban

Economics/politics 20
Case studies in government intervention and control of economy

Communication studies 21
CS of media development, for example, information and entertainment in contemporary Britain

Politics/ communication studies 22
Establishing a pressure group, for example, outsiders/ minorities

Futurology 23
Advanced technical societies, for example, California, Texas, Sweden, West Germany, Japan

Futurology 24
CS in Second Industrial Revolution — new technology and automation — social changes

History/ futurology 25
Development through time CS, for example, medicine, farming

Literature/ futurology 26
CS in science fiction — prediction of probability constraints

Sociology/ religious studies 27
'Cults of Unreason', for example, UFOs 'occult theories'

technique is the use of simulations which deliberately abstract the essence of systems and processes from the enormous complexity of the real world (see the accompanying diagram).

Particularly important areas of study are:

1 Technology and its effects on human life in a variety of contexts, which continues to provide the themes of many units, particularly the studies of recent developments in the local region, and also in the Third World. These themes are particularly related to development studies as an increasingly important field of study.

2 Many of the basic ideas are concerned with the rather misleading term 'global village'. This term relates to the effect of advanced technology applied to communications and to human transport, as well as to many of the themes that are prominent in this particular phase; many themes are concerned with the resolution of human conflict.

3 Many ideas are concerned with social and economic inequalities, particularly amongst nations or whole regions of the world, as well as of communities in geographical proximity. These studies of inequalities focus not only on the reasons for the uneven distribution of resources and opportunities, but also attempts at their resolution or diminution. Some of the units are concerned with political and social revolutions and others with developing technologies that we might assume to be important in the future.

4 Many ideas are necessarily concerned with the implications of the growth of mass societies apart from those already mentioned, particularly with the enormous pressure on the limits of the earth's resources and also with the psychological pressures on individual identity.

5 Some units are concerned with the attempts by groups and individuals at the planning, prediction and explanation of the human present and future. This 'explains' the units concerned with the development of new cities as well as with the emergence of some of the less rational ideologies or belief systems of the present time.

Here are appended some additional notes on particular units but not with any real hope of covering more than a fraction of the issues involved. However, these may be helpful to indicate my own thinking on the essential elements of these units and the linkages amongst them. It would be wrong to suppose that there is a link between every unit and every other unit in the course; but for the most part there are linkages although they may not appear directly between units that are roughly in the same numerical sequence. I give an example of one linkage which may not be immediately apparent, although there are many others. This concerns Phase Two where there are a number of units that appear to have very little in common. In practice what runs through many of the units is my own pre-occupation with people at the 'survival stage' in providing for their basic needs through food producing systems; most of the communities recommended for study in Phase Two are essentially small scale groups 'close to the soil'. These range from the earlier phase of the Greek city state which in pre-Hellenic times was certainly very small, through to the surveys of the local village, whether a rural or encapsulated village in the local area, to 'simple' farming systems, for instance in Texas or in West Africa, and again to the 'island theme'. Nearly all of the communities that are studied here are essentially small in scale. They are concerned with primary production and with using a relatively unsophisticated technology to produce basic materials.

Notes on Curriculum Unit Themes

Phase One

Unit A4

There needs to be some caution in the treatment of this theme as it deals with particularly sensitive issues as does the very last theme in Phase Four, that is 'Cults of unreason'. I would advise that superstitions are treated as the evidence of the persistence of folklore and that they are examined in order to provide valuable evidence of the survival of magical beliefs and as the basis of a considerable amount of ritual behaviour. It is likely that pupils will derive a great deal of entertainment and amusement from some of this work.

Unit A5

The outline for treatment of family history cannot improve on the advice in Steel and Taylor's hand-book *Family History in Schools*, which I would strongly recommend, in that there are all the techniques of research and presentation explained together with the necessary caveats about personal sensitivity.

Units A6 and A9

Most of the material needed for these units, which mainly deal with the local area, can be obtained from a variety of sources although this still needs to be extended. There is a great deal of material (cartographic, documentary and photographic) available in the local communities, from the libraries, from the County Records Offices, from the Geography and History departments in local colleges, and from local government offices.

Units A8 and A12

I am assuming in these units that mythology is at least of as much interest to the English and Arts departments in the school, or to the English and art teachers, as it is to the teachers of the humanities. Teachers of English and art who give particular prominence to the themes of mythology may make it unnecessary for these units to be dealt with more than briefly in the Humanities Department. Obviously my concern is that as mythology, with all its associations with religious beliefs and historical perceptions, is so important, that these themes should not be ignored.

Units A10 and A11

Both of these units, and indeed the other units on earth science, really demand a strong visual presentation and, if it is at all possible for children to go to the Science Museum and the Geological Museum, the opportunity should be taken. Even if it is not practical to arrange school visits there is sufficient material made available from the school sections of these museums for the children perhaps to use the opportunity in school holiday time.

Units A17 and A18

Like units A6 and A9, this material still needs to be established in most schools, although some are already quite well equipped with appropriate resources. If a number of people are interested in exploring the resource provision for these units in detail there is no reason why a group of teachers should not directly approach the County Planning Department and the other local government departments for the great range of maps, plans, photographs and statistical material they have available. Schools themselves can help considerably by establishing resource banks based on abstracts or extracts from newspapers, magazines such as the *County Magazines*, local directories, and local bus and railway timetables.

Phase Two

Units B1, B2 and B7

There is a good collection of material in most public libraries and many Teachers Centres on themes from the classical world. There is also outstandingly useful school materials produced by the Cambridge School Classics Project.

Units B3, B4 and B5

There are a number of excellent handbooks on village study techniques, many of them related to particular geographical areas. There is also a great deal of excellent fiction and autobiographical material on the recent past in rural life. Apart from the museums which are noted in the chapter on resources, there are good photographic collections both in published form, for many areas and, there has been a lot of very good television material both in school and adult programmes. A prime example of the presentation of life in the recent past is the television series *How we Used to Live*.

Units B8, B14 and B16

Many geography text books have excellent material, very often supported by filmstrips from publishers, on farming communities of the types specified here, but, nevertheless, there is a need to build up rather better coordinated case-study material. One of the things that appear in relatively few books, and would need to be acquired in some cases, are large-scale map extracts of special areas; for instance, the American West, the Australian Outback, West Africa and so on. Some farm studies, apart from those of the British Isles, are available from the Association of Agriculture and these are well worth obtaining if teachers have a particular interest in farming in certain other areas of the world.

Units B12 and B13

The Island Theme has been worked out in detail in a number of LEAs, and references to this form of approach will be found in a number of journals concerned with education, particularly journals such as *Forum, Teaching Geography* and *Teaching History*. There is an obvious parallel development in the use in English lessons of the voluminous literature on the theme of English families or individuals marooned on desert islands. One can approach the Island Theme through a number of techniques; some people will prefer, for instance, to deal with the climate, vegetation, 'natural disasters' aspect of 'island life' before looking at political organization and the need to provide from scarce resources. Many people suggest that one of the most useful techniques is to look at island analogies and fortunately there is a considerable amount of material on some rather small, obscure, islands such as Easter Island and Tristan de Cunha. One of the richest sources of information is one of the more bizarre inheritances from the British Empire; that is the large number of small island communities represented in the Commonwealth.[1] The Commonwealth Institute produces a great deal of material on these small communities; in fact, any community that has had a British connection is well documented.

Unit B19

This is a rather difficult topic to present without very good visual aids and models, but a search in the Science Department — particularly in some of the material from Schools Council projects — may reveal not only very good pictorial presentations in some of the text books but a list of appropriate visual aids included to develop understanding of these processes.

Phase Three

Units C2, and C3

Many of the earth science themes can produce polarized extremes of response. Some of the most bored children I have encountered have been learning the earth science aspects of geography; others have been intrigued by the concept of the changing surface of the earth. The problem is to find not only film material but adequate simulation material to show processes. Here again, the most effective way to do this is by a small group of schools working together in order to discuss the provision of simulation models which can be shared amongst the schools. These models could effectively show such varying processes as river development and the formation of the landscape.

Units C4 and C5

In a 'global village' world there is still a great over-emphasis on the western viewpoint on human behaviour; in order to redress the balance of the Judaeo-Hellenic heritage it is necessary to promote the idea that civilization does not equate with westernization and that not only peoples in different parts of the world have reached a high level of civilization, (some might claim a higher level than that attained in the West) but that they have produced societies that are viable on quite different suppositions from those which have developed from the roots of Palestine and Greece. However, because of the need to ruthlessly select from the units that I have listed here as worthy of attention, some people may prefer to use units C4 and C5 as extension or enrichment studies related to units B1, B2 and B7. One of the particular values of these units is to take the cross-cultural dimension in studying European expansion; B15 and B20 are concerned, partially at least, with the expansion of the Europeans across the globe and it may be a salutary experience to try to look at the Europeans through the eyes of the Africans, the Native Americans or the Polynesians.

Units C6, C8 and C9

Like the other units in the earth science section these can provide difficulties as most Humanities Departments are very often ill-equipped to carry out what is really a form of scientific research. There are, nevertheless, a number of study kits and books available from a variety of organizations that describe how to study the ecological pattern of coasts and of sea-shore life, or how to take samples of rocks and minerals. Humanities teachers may need a considerable amount of help from teachers of science. Undoubtedly this is a very rewarding subject of study but it needs a great deal of preparation and there are various strategies for taking some shortcuts in the provision of appropriate materials. As undoubtedly some of this work could have a school-holiday orientation, it is particularly important to provide children with the skills as well as the basic resources in order to carry out individual studies.

Units C10, C13, C15 and C16

These units are all concerned with transport and here I would suggest considerable use can be made of environmental resources in the locality. Transport studies, because they deal with complex interacting processes, are most effectively learned by an induction into a 'system' by the use of simulations; there are excellent simulations already available with such self-explanatory titles 'motorway' and 'developort'. Those schools which can manage long distance visits have great advantages in being able to take children to national museums with an emphasis on transport.

Units C12 and C14

All these units would depend on visits either from the school or by individual children. To obtain some flavour of what England was like in the early Industrial Revolution there is no substitute for a visit to a museum like the 'complex' at Ironbridge Gorge. Other textile, iron and mining museums are in the process of being developed in many parts of England and are described in numerous local and national guidebooks.

Units C20 and C21

Here there is an obvious opportunity for using studies in the local area. Most counties and regions with an industrial heritage can provide opportunities for research into the origins and development of local manufacturing enterprises.

For many people the service industries will hold as much interest and fascination as manufacturing industries; many medium-sized and large towns provide good examples of the new type of shopping centre and also of large-scale office developments.

Units C17, C18 and C22

All of these units are concerned with the use and development of holiday and leisure facilities, which is one of the three basic themes chosen by one of the best known School Council Projects designed for the upper secondary schools: this is the Avery Hill Project and the title of the particular theme is 'Man, land and leisure'. The development of the English seaside resort is a theme of perennial interest and so is that of the English-used holiday resort on the Mediterranean littoral. There is a great deal of material already available and the topic is highly appropriate for a long term simulation showing the development of a variety of leisure orientated communities.

Phase Four

Units D1, D2, D3, D4 and D5

The intensive study of urbanization is quite deliberate here although, of course, many of the units that I have recommended will be more appropriate for study in the upper secondary years. There is now an enormous amount of material on towns and town life in the nineteenth and twentieth centuries, easily located by the use of the *Yearbook of Urban History*. There are large 'banks' of photographic material and many museums have focussed particularly on town life in the nineteenth and early twentieth centuries. One of the essential themes promoted in these units is the idea of 'urbanness' in the concentration of facilities, the competition for resources, and the great diversity of urban forms, from that of the developed city in the westernized society to that of rapid metropolitan growth in Asia, Africa and Latin America.

Units D7 to D17

This series of studies focusses on the difficult issues of conflict and cooperation. Most of the units are more suitable for study by pupils in the upper secondary years, but although a careful selection has been made from the great mass of historical material which is also of interest to sociologists and economists, there are still many vital themes which all children should encounter. Of particular interest are the relationships between the individual and mass society, and the associated 'pressure to conformity', as well as the theme of the 'countervailing conscience', that is, individuals caught between two rival demanding systems such as Church and State. Particularly fruitful here are the links with drama, as human conflict has so much naturally dramatic appeal.

Some of the most useful links with drama are exemplified in the works of dramatists like Berthold Brecht, in such plays as *Mother Courage* and *Galileo*, in the work of Jean Giraudoux in *Tiger at the Gates*, in many of the works of Ibsen and in many of Shakespeare's plays concerned with the English monarchy and the ancient world. Some of the units deliberately pose some awkward, embarrassing, questions by illuminating incompatible perspectives on change and social conformity; for example, one unit, D3, is concerned with crime in its cultural context. Study of this unit theme may suggest that what is defined as crime may vary not only from place to place — for example, from Sicily to Switzerland — but also varies from social class to social class. Other units could easily pose the questions of what is meant by 'treason', 'patriotism' and 'martyrdom'.

Units D3, D6, D18 and D19

Many of the units have an emphasis on welfare geography, that is 'Who gets what and where', so that they pose the problems of why resources are so unequally distributed not only across the world but also in localities or regions, and give an insight into the problems of the development of settlements, communications and employment as well as their respective decline. These units are also concerned with what we mean by 'human rights' in its material connotation.

Units D21 and D22

These units pose questions concerning the roles and the rights of the individual in mass society; in other words, as the previous group of units was concerned with the basic needs of individuals in modern society, in a material sense, these are concerned with basic psychological and personal needs and constraints.

Units D23, D24, D25, D26 and D27

All these units have in common a focus on the future, as I believe that humanities, as much as the sciences, can make a special contribution to this area of vital concern. What one would hope is that there would be a more reasoned consideration of what are feasible future developments rather than the sort of 'space opera' type presentations in the earlier forms of science fiction. A lot of modern science fiction is quite invaluable for describing possible alternative futures and of facing some of the awkward but fundamental problems about the limitation and depredation of the earth's natural resources, whether the exploitation of the last great rain forest in the world, that of the Amazon, or the over-exploitation of the products of the soil or of the fossil fuels. An essential study is that of the shift from employment in manufacturing to the processing of data in the wake of computer-based information technology. The issues produced by the social effects of the introduction of the new technology have received little emphasis in many English schools in spite of the impact that this, and the associated decline in traditional manufacturing, have had on juvenile unemployment.

The final unit in the Futurology series, 'Cults of unreason', needs treating with some delicacy because there are likely to be some children who are in families which subscribe to these particular cults. However these seem to be particularly worth examining because many of them have bizarre but, nevertheless, seductively attractive versions of reality and reinterpretations of the past.

Note

1 See a recent account by S. Winchester (1985) *Outposts*, Hodder and Stoughton.

Chapter 9

Resources

Many of schools have developed quite complex forms of resource organization and here I might introduce one particular caveat, particularly as ancillary staff are difficult to find and to provide in even the largest schools. The caveat is simply that in the end the effectiveness of a resource system must be judged by the extent to which it facilitates the learning of the real clientele; that is the pupils in school. Some resource systems have been designed for undergraduate and postgraduate research and, when applied in a school system, have been usually ineffective. One tends to underestimate the difficulties of children operating a complex resource indexing system such as the Optical Coincidence System or other systems that depart far from the expectations and experience that children have. Nevertheless, the increasing use and application of computer-based information systems has immediate relevance in the use of, and access to, humanities resources.

It would be reasonable to expect, despite all the many reservations that resource specialists have about the Dewey Decimal System, that most, by the end of the early secondary years, should have a working knowledge of how this system operates. In other words they should be familar with the 'First Summary' of Dewey, understand the way the Dewey System classifies material, and be aware of its limitations. There are particular difficulties in the humanities, as illustrated in table 6 showing the variety of classifications that might be appropriate in a humanities scheme. There are also particular problems about access, storage and retrieval with mixed media resources. Obviously, the situation is much easier when one is concerned only with books in the library, or even books and other printed materials, but if one considers the great diversity of resource materials and their particular presentation needs, then obviously some basic problems have to be solved. There are now many schools that have already given deep consideration to these problems and have found a number of ingenious solutions to providing a resource system rather than a conventional school library.

Table 6: Library — Humanities in 'Dewey'

A Few 'humanities' sections in 'Dewey'

030	Encyclopaedias	
070	Journalism	X
160	Logic	
170	Ethics	
270	Christian history	X
290	Other religions	X
300	Social science	
310	Statistics	X
320	Politics	X
330	Economics	X
340	Law	X
350	Public administration	X
360	Social welfare	X
380	Commerce	X
390	Customs	X
519	Statistics	
526	Mathematical geography	
550	Earth science	
570	Anthropology	X
608	Inventions	
613–4	Health, Safety	X
620	Engineering	
630	Agriculture	X
660	Industrial chemistry	X
670	Manufactures	
710	Town planning	X
720	Architecture	X
759	Historical painting	X
782	Dramatic music	X
784	Vocal music	X
791	Cinema	X

All of 800 —

All of 900 —

(X Modern World Study)

Central to the effective use of resources in whatever form is the training in learning skills. One of the more bizarre by-products of the assumptions that some people held in the late 1960s and early 1970s, was a belief that the teacher was only the facilitator for children craving knowledge and understanding. This always seemed to have an element of completely false romanticism about it but, even more dangerously, the proponents of this unsubstantiated theory very often did not ensure that effective study skills were learned. Notoriously many pupils in the fourth and fifth years of secondary schools, and certainly a high proportion in the sixth-forms, have never been taught to study effectively. This lies at the root of many of the problems that students, whether as pupils in schools or in colleges, or as adults, still suffer. Effective use of school resources can only be obtained if children are systematically taught how to study in the broadest sense. There are now a number of good handbooks on this, which are referred to in the bibliography, but many of them seem to assume that study skills only need to be taught in the post-sixteen phase of education. At the root of many of our problems is this failure to train children in effective use of books and non-book materials, in basic skills such as notetaking, cross-referencing, indexing, fast reading, and so on.

Skills in Humanities (Adapted from *Time, Place and Society*)

Cognitive

1 Intellectual
   (a) Find information from variety of sources
   (b) Present information in variety of forms
   (c) Interpret and evaluate
   (d) Test hypotheses — generalize
2 Social
   (a) Participate in variety of groups
   (b) Understand group/society relations
   (c) Empathize
3 Physical
   (a) Expressive skills
   (b) Use equipment

Affective

Moral and aesthetic awareness — curiosity, scepticism, potentiality, open-mindedness.

Study Skills

Derek Rowntree's recommendation for the treatment of a textbook is the following, in five main stages: (significantly the same basic method can be applied to film-strip, video-cassette or computer disc)

1 *Survey*
   The student is asked to make a very brief survey of the content of the textbook by using the table of contents,

chapter headings, the index and reference system, in order to gain a general understanding of what is the concern of the particular book and what are its limitations.

2 *Question*
Here the student is looking at the book as a source of what specific information or insights or approaches he needs himself for his particular task, considering in what form he wishes to present the information that he has acquired, and how the elements of information would be related to other courses, whether in terms of information from other books or from non-book materials.

3 *Read*
Here the instruction is to read for a particular purpose and obviously there must be training in effective fast reading by learning the techniques of faster reading described in a number of books. Basically the process is that of extending the visual span, skimming for particular information and looking for 'key words' and 'key ideas' particularly if these are presented in some visual form.

4 *Recall*
This is a matter of breaking down the printed material, in this case the textbook, into sections, and making notes on the particular matters of concern to the student. Here again there is a need for a considerable amount of guidance on the exposition of arguments, or the representation of processes.

5 *Review*
What the student is trained to do here is to check back on the whole process and look at the implications for the next stage of his research.

Obviously this five stage process of 'Survey, Question, Read, Recall, Review' is not learned immediately, or even during the period of a year or two years; it is a continuous learning process of how to study applied to virtually all the sorts of learning stimuli that the student encounters.

One central problem about the provision of resources in schools is of severe limitations on expenditure. The capitation allowances, and the extra sources of revenue that many schools have found, are seldom adequate to provide for all the school needs. Here one is up against some hard facts of school administration. It has been alleged, quite feasibly, that a 5 per cent saving on teachers' salaries could produce a 90 per cent increase in resource expenditure on books, stationery and materials. This element of virement is not open to the schools in most authorities so the obvious lesson is to make the most effective use of resources in schools as they presently exist.

A modern school resource centre has a great variety of materials to be used and these can be briefly scheduled as including at least some in the following list, apart from the obvious features such as reference books and textbooks in the school library or in the classroom. It emphasizes, however, the difficult problems about deciding on the demarcation between pupil and teacher access to materials and particularly the problem of deciding what is a reasonable medium stage between a system where there is completely open access to all materials by the users and a very restricted, limited access for pupils and even for some of the teaching staff. Obviously, one has to take account of the great cost, complexity and sensitivity of the more expensive forms of hardware, and indeed, even of some of the software. I have in mind particularly the great expense involved in the ineffectual, or dangerous, use of machines such as video-cassette recorders or photocopying machines. Nevertheless, the acquisition by many families of equipment such as computers and video-cassette recorders has resulted in a situation in which many children are likely to be more adept and knowledgeable about the use of electronic hardware than their schoolteachers.

Some of the materials that one might expect to find in a centre are the following:

(a) Audio-cassettes and video-cassettes or tapes.
(b) Computer discs and cassettes, unless these are kept in a 'computer-base'.
(c) Slides for projection, in a number of forms extending from the overhead projector slide, which may be under-used in a number of schools (particularly if there is no effective OHP 'production programme') through to the much used 35mm slides, either acquired from commercial sources or produced by staff or pupils. One of the most effective forms of presentation is one to which I have alluded previously in this handbook, that is of a combination of the C60 or C90 audio-cassette with the 'bank' of 35mm colour slides.
(c) Maps, charts and other large paper-borne materials. A number of schools have made very successful devices for storage and retrieval systems for these rather cumbersome and often expensive materials.
(d) Kits and study aids, which may range from SRA 'Do It Yourself' learning kits to the great variety of package kits emanating from Schools Council Projects and from 'independent' publishers. One particular note I think should be made about the use of kits. There have been a few cases where schools have rather rashly misused a kit which has taken a great deal of time, expertise and money in assemb-

ling and collating diverse elements; because the resource centre is extremely influential in the school, the elements in the kit, instead of being kept together, have been disintegrated and catalogued under a variety of classifications.

(e) Games and simulations — these are very often presented in kit form but they may have particular storage needs, for example, for simulations that use large board materials; there are some games, such as the Coca-Cola Game, which concentrate on alternative use of environmental resources, and are not easily stored in the way suitable for most of the kits which can be packed into boxes.

(f) Magazines and journals — many schools have been forced to discontinue the purchase of these, but there are other ready sources, particularly if it is not crucial that one has to have this week's or this month's particular magazine. There is a great variety of journals that could be put into effective use in schools when children can bring them from home (presumably after the other members of the family have had the necessary use from them).

There are already some quite complex total resource systems developed, particularly by some of the larger authorities. Amongst the most notable of these is the Avon Resources for Learning Development Unit, which presents packages, mostly of printed material but also of some other material such as film strips and slides and cassettes. There has been a similar development in London which has a network of Media Resource Centres and, here again, not only complete kits have been produced, but also complete systems which interrelate printed materials and audio-visual materials. The most notable development, apart from those of some of the larger LEAs, for our particular purpose in humanities, is the Longman's Group 'Resources Unit', which works on a form of subscription system. Further information on this can be obtained from the publishers.

The handbooks mentioned in the bibliography outline the formidable argument for the development of resource-based learning in schools, but it may well be appropriate to summarize the key reasons adduced by the teachers and educationalists who have looked into the needs of schools.

The organization of resource-based learning is the key to many issues.

Firstly, by considering all the resources in the school and outside that are relevant to the study of a particular topic or issue, it makes for a much more coordinated development of the curriculum and seeks out the strategies by which the reinforcement of learning may be effected. One looks for similar 'concerns' from a number of disciplines and curricular areas and for the more effective use of materials rather than only in one particular section of the curriculum.

Secondly, the effective development of a resource-based system is an economic advantage in that effective use should be made of all school resources and, as part of this process, internal resources will be identified and made specific, and thereby the school will make more effective the identification of its needs to be obtained from outside. This development relates closely to the need for a continuous content analysis which can be greatly facilitated by the expression of all schemes of work in a modular form.

Thirdly, it provides for more effective individual learning, particularly on the assumption that children will experience a variety of classroom situations, from formal lessons at one extreme, to a considerable amount of group and individual work, where at least individual children have the opportunity to exercise an element of choice, not only in the subjects which they pursue but also in the way they pursue them. If the needs of slow learners and fast learners are identified, the resource system can make much more effective provision for the individual needs of these pupils. The need of gifted children for enrichment materials is briefly considered in another section (see the note at the end of chapter 10).

There are many examples of physically handicapped children overcoming learning problems by the effective use of teacher guidance combined with the best use of resources. The problem of providing adequate resources for the fast learning children is a taxing one.

In working out the specific needs for the extension materials for the curriculum units described in this handbook, the most effective method is likely to be by setting up a number of working groups, amongst teachers in schools, to consider ways in which each unit can provide greater depth of learning for the children who constitute this minority of the population. In general the assumption is that enrichment material will be built into each unit with a study guide 'annexe' for the gifted children to use. Occasionally it should be possible to use one of the other units which is not being used by the whole cohort of children and which is conceptually related to the main unit. A good example would be the use of unit A8 for the whole group and the use of unit A12 for the gifted pupils, or B10 for the whole group and B15 for the gifted pupils; however it is important to bear in mind that these units, when used with gifted pupils, should be used in a different way from that of the conventional use provided for the whole cohort.

Fourthly, curriculum units, as described in the handbook, can be much more effectively coordinated by a resource-based learning system, in that the linkages become apparent and the particular as well as the common needs of the units are relatively easily identified. As mentioned previously it is far easier to integrate 'local' resources produced in unit form with the resources offered by outside agencies. Experience seems to suggest that there can be a considerable diversity in effective provision of storage and retrieval systems. The most important factor to consider is not whether the storage and retrieval system is centrally held for the use of the whole school, but the effectiveness of the cross-referencing system and the location index, so that it should be possible to identify what the school possesses as well as external resources where each element or artefact is specified by its location.

Fifthly, resource unit elements have a variety of reasons for their inclusion and this has implications for teaching strategies. For example, a particular element may be there simply to stimulate the interests of the children, may be there to provide an induction into a process or a system, may provide guidance on study techniques or study sequences. An element may be there for the reinforcement of learning initiated at an earlier stage, or may be there for the purpose of showing the variety of information and presentation by which learning can be stimulated.

A resource index should show the following information:

1 The form in which the information is held, for example whether it is in the form of a book, a building outside the school, a film, a study pack, or even a person who is a particular source of valuable information.

2 Location — it should show where the element is stored, for instance in the school audio-visual store, in a Teachers Centre, the School Library Service, a museum, a particular building.

3 The date of origin — this may be of crucial importance in using up-to-date material for humanities, or if not using up-to-date material, to have an awareness of the relative degree of obsolescence so that one can make an appropriate adjustment for this factor.

4 It is desirable to have some rough chronological classification which could range reasonably from pre-history to the future, 'by way of' the Bronze Age, the Iron Age, the ancient world, medieval times, early modern times, and so forth.

5 Similarly there should be a topographical reference (see figure 00 on page 00) which could range from a district or village, for example, through the local town, the countries of Europe, to the non-European world and 'outer space'.

Perhaps the most important feature of the indexing system is:

6   Topics or features lists — good examples of these lists can be had from many of the handbooks and resources centres. Particularly useful ones are those given in chapter 5 of R P Edwards' book (1973) *Resources in Schools* and Holdern and Mitson's book, (1974) *Resources Centres*, chapter 3. If one took some of the features that would be first in alphabetical order, they are the following:
Advertising, Agriculture, Air, Amphibians, Animals, Anthropology, Archaeology, Architecture, Armed forces, The arts, Astronomy, Atomic, Attitudes, Authority.

Outdoor Resources and Visits

The pattern recommended for environmental work is that set down by Lines and Bolwell (1971) in the *Teachers Handbook to Environmental Studies*. A similar work, although orientated towards urban studies, is that by Colin Ward and Tony Fyson (1973) entitled *Streetwork*. For up-to-date information there is one invaluable journal published every month called *The Bulletin of Environmental Education*. Back copies of this are available in a number of libraries and educational institutions; this is a compendium of all aspects of environmental work, but particularly strong is the work that has been the preoccupation of the journal in recent years, that is the aesthetic approach to the urban environment. In the Bulletin of Environmental Education there will be found a large number of town trails which may well act as models for developing town trails in the local area.

There have been two Schools Council Projects directly concerned with the environment, the Environmental Studies Project 5–13, and 'Project Environment', which looks at the more general issues of approaches to environmental study. The Environmental Studies Project 5–13 has produced four particularly useful volumes; a *Teachers Handbook*, a small compendium of *Case Studies* and two larger format books, *Starting from Rocks* and *Starting from Maps*. There is now a huge wealth of material available on resources for environmental work. One might mention, for example, Shire Publications for its extensive *Discovering* series. The main reference, of course, for all aspects of environmental education is the coordinating agency, the Council for Environmental Education, to which reference is made later in this chapter. For the necessary preparation and the logistics of educational visits, the most useful publication is that of the Schools Council (1976) called *Out and About*, published by Evans/Methuen.

Museums

There are a number of basic references, the most important of which is the annually produced ABC guide *Museums and Galleries in Great Britain and Ireland*. However, this has the obvious weakness of only giving outline information and, perhaps far more useful for many people, are the guides produced by many Teachers Centres. Some centres have both produced *Where to Go* handbooks, which list not only museums, but historic houses, castles, zoological gardens and so on. There are many museums that would serve the needs of people studying particular units suggested in this handbook. Examples would be the following:

(a) For conflict studies or military studies, there are in many areas locally accessible museums concerned with specific battles, but for both World Wars obviously the major resource is the Imperial War Museum in London.

(b) Recent years have seen the growth of rural life museums, some of which may be feasible for a day visit, although of outstanding value for children who may be visiting in the area. As East Anglia is such a popular region for 'home-based' holidays, it might well be worth noting the museum of rural life at Stowmarket, but there are many others of excellent quality from Durham to Cornwall.

(c) There are a number of museums that are particularly concerned with vernacular buildings and also with home life. Two might merit particular attention for those studying the changes in domestic life and in buildings over the centuries. One which concentrates on vernacular buildings as such is the Avoncroft Open Air Museum near Bromsgrove in Worcestershire, and in London the Geffrye Museum, which has a particular concern with the educational approach to understanding changes in domestic life. A number of city museums, mainly in the north of England, have replications of Victorian streets, shops and houses. Particularly notable are those at York, Salford and Leeds.

(d) There is a separate publication dealing with transport museums, but ones that would be of particular interest to children in relevant curriculum units are those such as the Railway Museum at York and the Tramway Museum at Crich in Derbyshire.

(e) In the last decades a number of museums have been developed to show the early years of the Industrial Revolution and, of course, this is a fundamental theme in a number of the curriculum units. Perhaps the outstanding one is the

Open Air Industrial Museum at Ironbridge in Shropshire, which shows the very beginnings of the Industrial Revolution and is now really a complex of interrelated museums rather than a single museum. Of similar interest are the recently opened Gladstone Museum at Longton in The Potteries, which illustrates one of the most famous of British industries and the open-air museum complex at Beamish in Durham.

(f)   Many towns have now developed in their museums specific sections dealing with the growth of their own communities. Books which are referred to in the bibliography but which may be cited now, in view of their particular relevance, are: Alexander, E (1974) *Museums and How to Use Them*; Fairley, J (1972) *History Teaching through Museums*; Schools Council *Pterodactyls and Old Lace*

All of these give a considerable amount of advice on the necessary preparation and the most effective use of museums. I should mention briefly here the great variety of the curriculum units that are published by individual museums. Of particular use are the following:

(i)   from the Imperial War Museum — the material on oral history related to the two World Wars;

(ii)   from the Science Museum — a great variety of relatively cheap and well illustrated publications on such themes as the development of all sorts of machinery but particularly textile machinery and transport;

(iii) from the Geological Museum — very useful publications such as *The Story of the Earth* and *Britain Before Man*, as well as a range of wall charts;

(iv)   from the Victoria and Albert Musuem — a great diversity of publications from the museum itself, and from other sources, on the classical world and oriental civilizations. Similar publications are available from the British Museum;

(v)   the Natural History Museum has developed a very strong section on ecology in recent years and two of their publications are invaluable for both teacher and pupil, *Understanding Ecology* and *Nature at Work*.

Major Interest Groups

Some curricular areas have shown such extraordinary development in the last decade that it is now very difficult to specify all the materials available or even the organizations directly concerned. It may help to mention simply three of these, although there are many more. Firstly, the group concerned with *European Studies*, which in practice may be a misleading title in that the focus is on Western Europe and particularly on the 'European Economic Community'.

The major source of information on the European organizations is a handbook available from the Department of Education and Science which has collated a great deal of information in one publication called *International Understanding: Sources of Information on Organisations: A Handbook for Schools and Colleges.* Another organization concerned particularly with Europe itself is the Centre for Contemporary European Studies at the University of Sussex. Publications available from this institution include the *European Studies Handbook* and its supplements. There is also an organization called the European Communities Information Service with its headquarters at 20 Kensington Palace Gardens, London W8, which publishes catalogues of organizations and sources of information on the EEC.

Environmental Education

As previously mentioned, the main source of information here is the Council for Environmental Education based at the University of Reading School of Education. This organization has published a number of useful guides to resources in environmental education; particularly useful for schools is the *Directory of Environmental Literature and Teaching Aids.* Of particular interest to such schools are the numerous plans and reports available from County and District Planning Offices. These can include special studies of conservation areas, reports on urban redevelopment, structure plans, transport programmes, as well as official guides to whole counties as well as districts. Many areas now have urban trails, heritage trails for countryside villages and towns as well as schedules of listed buildings and archaeological sites.

Particularly useful approaches are to be found in Department of the Environment Design Bulletins such as *The Estate Outside the Dwelling* which introduces criteria for the measurement of 'liveability' and the convenience of flats and houses in relation to amenities such as privacy, car-parking, shopping, security and others such as living 'high up' or close to the ground.

Development Studies or Third World Studies

(a) There are a number of handbooks; a General Handbook and separate ones on China, Japan and Africa from the School of

Oriental and African Studies (Extramural Division) at the University of London.

(b) The basic coordinating organization is the Council for World Development Education, which produces an invaluable catalogue called *The Development Puzzle*. The address of this organization is 25 Wilton Road, London SW1.

(c) The Commonwealth Institute at Kensington High Street, which has an enormous range of publications dealing with general problems as well as with specific Commonwealth and ex-Commonwealth countries.

There are similar interest groups for American studies where particular reference would be to the American Museum at Bath, to the Institute of American Studies at the University of Exeter, and to the American Studies Centres at Manchester and Central London polytechnics. Urban studies is 'represented' in a number of universities, amongst them the University of Leicester, which has considerable material on the history and sociology of urban areas and publishes the essential *Year Book of Urban Studies*.

The Popular Media as a Resource

I have already suggested that many schools ignore the popular media either consciously or unconsciously. I would see a basic requirement of the schools to produce an informed, critical audience and readership for the media, whether television, radio, magazine or popular fiction; the emphasis in schools should be on the effective use of media as a source of information and particularly in developing a critical faculty and awareness of all that children encounter in the 'extra curriculum' which is being presented to them.

Audio-Visual Materials and Reprographics

I am only making a brief reference to this matter here, as there is so much specific advice on this from organizations such as NCVAE and the Council for Educational Technology, and because there are particular technical problems as well as the financial problems in setting up an effective audio-visual and reprographic system. There are two basic needs to be met; firstly effective projection of sound and pictures, and secondly the reproduction of materials. (One should bear in mind the restrictions imposed by the Copyright Law; it is important to note that Copyright restrictions apply to both the copying of printed materials as well as their reproduction in other forms, and also to the recording of sound and vision, whether from broadcast, record or film.)

Most secondary schools appear to concentrate on particular forms of media projection, and experience of most secondary schools and middle schools suggests that four types of projection and recording apparatus should meet most needs.

(a) Most important is access to colour television both directly or, more usefully, by the use of the video-cassette recorder. The recorder obviously allows for curricular time specification and allows the school to use the television programmes as they relate to its needs in particular curricular units rather than be 'forced' to use television at a 'difficult' time or a programme which might be inappropriate for the main work in process.

(b) I should perhaps call attention to what appear to be a gross under-use of radio in many schools. Radio seems to me to have great advantages of liberating the imagination, being relatively cheap and easy to use and, where combined with the use of a cassette recorder and film slides or film strips, is quite as powerful a resource as television.

(c) Related to the use of radio is the use of the slide film projector and very often this can be most effectively used if it is accompanied by prepared cassettes. This also gives one of the most effective exchange systems with other schools, either in other parts of Britain or with other countries; that is the production of sets of 35mm colour slides accompanied by C60 or C90 cassette commentaries. This package can be sent relatively cheaply almost anywhere in the world and presents an instant case study of a British school in return for similar material from the country to which it has been despatched.

(d) The overhead projector again seems to be little used in a surprising number of schools, particularly in view of its versatility and the fact that with a little ingenuity it can replace many of the more cumbersome visual projectors which were used in the past. Particularly useful is the overhead projector with a prepared bank of materials in the form of overlays, which can supplement maps and time charts. This sort of system is particularly effective for full group teaching of a conceptual development and also for indicating a range of resources. The preparation of the OHP slides with the use of some photocopying machines can provide a most effective method of integrating pupil material with projected material.

(e) The 16mm film projector, although useful, has perhaps declined in use in many schools. Not only is there the problem of the high cost of obtaining film from other sources than the Authority Film Library, but the problem is also that so many films are not only expensive but very quickly become obsolete. However, the 16mm film projector does have a number of desirable features, particularly in the showing of film to large groups of pupils.

Reprographic Systems

Basic needs are for, firstly, cheap multiple copies of material for pupils produced in the form of booklets, and these are far more effectively supplied by groups of teachers preparing unit material than by attempted abstraction from other sources. It should be borne in mind that there is a need for quick, easily reproduced material, for instance by the manually operated duplicator, as well as for the production of material by the use of expensive, more complex machinery, such as the 'offset-litho-printer'. One of the problems of the development of worksheets in the last decade has been that very often relatively poor quality material has been produced, particularly because of the enthusiasm of schools which was not met by an equivalent provision of, or access to, high quality machinery and the necessary ancillary help. It is always advisable to use good quality commercially available materials before thinking of hand-produced material. The other need has already been suggested, that is of producing material in the form of worksheets or guidelines that directly relate the pupil material to the projector material, particularly as these can be produced in the form of overhead projector slides. This combination of OHP slide and pupil guideline is invaluable for introducing the use of particular enquiry techniques, for example in the use of statistics, documents, map reading skills, as well as to study basic processes and systems. Most worksheets could be markedly improved by better layout and illustrations with more diagrams and less small print, so that they have the character of study-guides rather than small-scale substitute textbooks.

The Use of Simulations

This has been one of the most misunderstood, misrepresented curriculum developments. In fact, one can look at a continuum in the use of simulations that extends from the case study, to exemplify a particular process or community, through role play to the participant game and, at its most abstract, ending with computer simulation. There has been a major growth in the use of simulations in schools as well as a national organization to suggest the most effective uses of simulation in learning. This is not to suggest that simulations should in any way replace other teaching techniques, but simply that simulations have an invaluable role to play in the induction of students into processes and systems.

The most effective use of simulations is in developing children's understanding of processes and systems, but there are other particular advantages that have been adduced by the proponents of simulations:

(a) Children are able to take on roles representing the real world and take part in the process of making judgments and of understanding the way decisions are formed. Good examples of this, and of examples of role change, will be in some of the games produced by the Longman's Resources Unit. A particularly good example would be the *Railway Game*, developed by Mr Rex Walford some ten years ago, which simulates the development of the American Transcontinental Railway System and obviously would be of direct use in a curriculum unit such as that on the American West.

(b) Children are able to see the consequence of their own performances as a result of decisions; that is the most effective part of many games is the 'post mortem'. Although children may not enjoy this process first of all, there is an invaluable opportunity to study a process of decision-making and implementation and measure its effects, and thereby to evaluate the judgments that have been made.

(c) Simulations are able to relate very closely to the Informal Curriculum. The extent of games played in children's playgrounds is still considerable, although perhaps not as evident as in the variety of games described by Peter and Iona Opie in previous decades. Nevertheless, many games relate closely to the informal educational processes that are going on, both at home and at school.

(d) An important characteristic is that simulation enables children to empathize with others, and this is seen most clearly in children playing games such as *Motorway*, which simulates the development of a motorway through an urban area with various groups extolling, criticizing and opposing the development; *Sunshine*, which is concerned with the effects of racial segregation and the allocation of resources in an American town; and *Star-Power*, which is a particularly penetrating appraisal of the distribution of economic resources in relation to the social class system.

(e) Simulations can make an understanding of what sounds to be a formidable concept, such as Industrial Location or The Friction of Distance, readily accessible to most children by the application of such concepts to 'life situations'.

(f) Simulations stress something that I am particularly concerned about: that is they emphasize the possible, rather than the already determined, in that in historical simulations, particularly, children are able to see that history is a combination of the deterministic and the 'serendipitous' and that many of the fundamental changes in history, especially political history, have hinged on the decisions made by particular individuals in particular situations.

(g) Simulations greatly extend the context of understanding, particularly as they refer to the relationships between the individual and the group in which the individual is working and living.

It is necessary to give a caution about the use of simulations; they are not necessarily a replacement for other forms of learning, and, unless the simulation is closely monitored and structured, it can be relatively unproductive both in the acquisition of skills and in the development of ideas.

Computer Assisted Learning

One major recent development in schools is the introduction of computers so that in many authorties virtually all secondary (and a very high proportion of primary schools) have computers.

There is a variety of popular computers in schools but it can be assumed that in most local authorities there is a standard computer provision for every school. Some schools may have acquired extra computers by various strategies and a number of them will have computer rooms equipped for the use of two dozen or so children at one time.

There are, however, particular problems about when computers can make an effective and imaginative contribution to learning and humanities and in what circumstances major improvements need to be effected in classroom organization to allow the computer to be used in the same imaginative way as has been accomplished in the use of some audio visual equipment.

The major developments that we may expect to see in the provision of computer software in the next few years should provide us with more interactive programmes with the facility to readily translate quantitative data into vivid diagramatic presentation and to rearrange data of varying types in a manner that would be accessible and useful to pupils.

At present many of the humanities programmes have only limited use for routine applications, such as the reinforcement of basic skills such as map reading, and the identification of specific features in the past or in topographical geography. More useful applications need to be shown in the form of analysis of data both diagrammatic and pictorial, for example in the census of a small area to show categories of age, occupation and mobility and to show their inter-relationships. This has already been achieved in a few local areas but the major problems are the writing in of the data base in a form where it can readily be used by teachers and pupils without highly specific training. Some other useful applications already developed illustrate and clarify decision-making processes and so produce an essential element in the learning of history and geography. That is they emphasize possibilism as against the determinism that is so often the product of a high reliance on text books. This the computer can do by reinterpreting actual events by a process called 'analogue theory' in which alternative developments and processes take place and thus allow measurement between alternative possibilities and reality.

Examples of some of the more interesting programmes, although all of these show the possibility of considerable improvement are the following:

(a) *Drake's Voyage*, which simulates the problems encountered in the mariner's voyage around the world where a number of encounters both with climatic factors as well as personal factors such as the mutiny of some of the crew provide the opportunity for the user to make decisions about how to proceed.

(b) *Population* is a programme which simulates population growth in a choice of countries. Interestingly the data is taken from the World Bank Atlas and the World Development Report. This programme could be amplified to relate to such other matters as gross national product and hence illuminate the North-South divisions described so impressively in the Brandt Report.

(c) *Village*, is concerned with a historical geography simulation on the location of a village in seventh century England. Here the simulation shows the relationship to the location of a village in its accessibility to essential resources and the use of 'efficiency ratings'. The problem is then posed of the real life decision which might often have been made between economic efficiency and the site that would be easily and adequately defended.

Other simulations presently available concern a variety of geographical and historical situations such as coastal erosion, population growth in the local area natural hazards such as population and flooding, the simulated growth of a town in the nineteenth century, the processes of overseas trading companies and environmental problems caused by motorway construction and airport location. Already the range of materials is sufficient to indicate some of the possibilities for improving the understanding of systems and processes. The 'quantum leap', however, is to produce more schools and pupils who are not dependent on particular software programmes but can begin to produce their own simulations and be feeding into the data base the sort of material that will enhance their understanding of processes. To achieve this there must be a more systematic attempt to approach some of the problems concerning classroom organization and, as the Schools Council 14–18 Geography Project team has suggested, there should be a reorientation towards a partnership model where the pupils and the teacher have direct access to the computer and where they use it as a valuable aid to understanding some of the main issues that are being studied.

The exploration of the local environment, whether in the past or the present, depends on the efficiency with which local authorities can make provision for the development and expansion of data bases containing locally useful material such as census data and the great variety of information available in County Record Offices and Planning Departments.

On a very practical classroom level not only do pupils need much more responsive interactive programmes but also 'video displays' which are more useful in the situation in which most children work, with the ability to change the scale and position on a visual display unit to present effectively a mix of types of information such as diagrams, text and perhaps most important of all to improve the readability of information on both screens and print outs.

From the stand point of early 1986 it seems that the potential of computer assisted learning in humanities has only just begun to appear. Nevertheless like good audio visual use we may assume that the use of the computer for enhanced classroom learning will be as good as the classroom organization and curriculum planning allows it to be. It is encouraging that good quality programmes produced for Tressell Publications and by the Exeter School of Education group have become available. Recourse should be made to the regional headquarters of the Micro-Electronics Project.

Chapter 10

Assessment and Evaluation

There is no doubt that assessment and evaluation is the most difficult and taxing part of designing a scheme of work or a major element in the curriculum. The difficulty has been enhanced by developments in the last few years and is shown in the great interest which has been expressed in the way schools assess pupil performance, and also in the evaluation of the curriculum that they are offering. Indications of this concern and interest are shown by both the activities of the Department of Education and Science at national level, in establishing the Assessment of Performance Unit (APU), and also by the recommendations of a number of government reports, amongst them, most conspicuously, has been the Taylor Report in its recommendation for the involvement of the governors of school in curriculum concerns. Implied in this is the assumption that schools are accountable not only to the local education authority, and more indirectly to the Department of Education and Science, but also are more directly accountable for pupil performance to the local community. This, of course, has always been implied, but until relatively recently has not been made so explicit by asking schools to account for not only competence in the basic skills of language and numeracy, but also for performance in external examinations.

We are now in a situation where education, as a major consumer of public expenditure, is seen by many people, not only those directly connected with the school, such as parents, governors, and local education authority officers, but also the community at large, in terms of measured pupil performance. Undoubtedly the rigidity of some assessment procedures has had a very inhibiting effect on curriculum development and this reflects perhaps the years of curriculum development and expansion that characterized the late 1960s and early 1970s where the emphasis was mainly on curriculum innovation and development, with relatively little account paid to effective pupil assessment procedures, or to course evaluation problems.

A great deal of effort, time and money may be expended in developing a curriculum innovation which, if strictly evaluated, may

Figure 24: Assessment — Basis

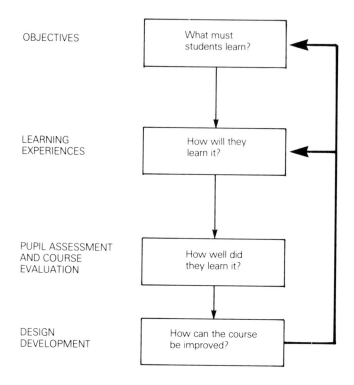

What are we trying to learn?

OBJECTIVES — What must students learn?

LEARNING EXPERIENCES — How will they learn it?

PUPIL ASSESSMENT AND COURSE EVALUATION — How well did they learn it?

DESIGN DEVELOPMENT — How can the course be improved?

be found not to serve the purposes which are stated as its objectives, and therefore not only are the course developers discouraged, but also there is the sad recognition that a considerable amount of experience and knowledge of developer, teacher and pupil, may well have been ineffectually used. The fundamental reason for situations like this, which are too numerous to record, is that in many cases the objectives of the course have not been specified in sufficient detail. The first essential procedure is to clarify learning objectives in describing what we expect pupils should be doing in school at a particular time, and what sort of features we should be looking for when we assess their progress. Someone has appropriately observed 'If we do not specify what we want, we have to put up with what we get'.

The inadequacy in spelling out objectives is reflected in a general vagueness about what the process of learning is and, because of this, the criteria which we have used for the success of the course very often have failed to do adequate justice to the course designers. Quite complicated assessment schemes based on knowledge-recall assessment procedures have been devised although perhaps the real intention of the curriculum plan has been to awaken awareness, to develop understanding, to induct pupils into skills or different ways of apprehending a field of knowledge. All these features of the course may well be missed out by a very limited testing or assessment procedure that simply concentrates on elements of memory recall of a small part of the curriculum. With these caveats in mind it may well be appropriate for the author to establish some working or operational definitions of the main terms used. 'Assessment', and 'evaluation' are used synonymously in many cases, but developing educational practice has tended to define them in the following ways.

'Assessment' is normally used for the process of the measurement of the quality and the quantity of learning over a period of time, whether by individual pupils or by groups. 'Evaluation', as the derivation of the word suggests, is concerned with the judgment of the value and effectiveness of the course as it is related to an assumed standard. In practice, the terms have to be used interchangeably in some senses because the only effective evaluation of a curriculum course in the last instance is by estimating its value to the students taking it. Although we may judge a course to be immaculate in theoretical terms, the fact that the pupils are unable to cope with the demands of the course, or make inadequate progress in terms of the standards which we have established, really devalues the course for most practical purposes.

The problems of assessment will be dealt with first of all, and then, at the end of this chapter, matters concerned with course evaluation. The basic components of assessment may be indicated by the following questions.

Firstly, what should the course do for students? What knowledge, skills and attitudes should they be acquiring? Secondly, how do we know whether the course has been successful or not? This indicates what sort of measurements we should apply to the course and the question of how we can weigh their relative effectiveness. This brings us to one of the central problems of assessment, that is, whether our concern is mainly to be with *criterion-referencing*: ('Are we assessing the course against an external standard — for instance, using a test set by the publishers of a course of text-book form, or standards set by external examining bodies?'), or are we looking at a *norm-referencing system* by which we intend to measure the progress of individual students compared with those of the other members of the group? The difference between the two methods might well be expressed in the following way: if a pupil is working well by norm-referenced standards she may gain 50 per cent of the overall assessment grading, whereas by criterion-referencing standards she may be gaining only 25 per cent. What this would indicate is that by national standards, or by some external standards, the general performance of the group of which the particular pupil is a member, is relatively low.

What is being emphasized is that unless we are quite clear about our objectives beforehand — of what we hope the course will do for the pupils — there is little point in devising assessment procedures. This also raises the fundamental question of 'What are the purposes of assessment?' These may be classified as shown table 7 so we are concerned with a variety of reasons for measuring individual pupil progress. If we have a degree of clarity about this (and this is only a very brief list of reasons for pupil-assessment and needs to be 'thrashed out' in more detail) then we may well turn our attention to the characteristics of an effective assessment programme. I have already alluded to the fact that much of what passes for assessment in many schools is concerned with a very limited range or part of the overall course objectives, and this in a sense does grave injustice to the designers of the course and to the teachers and pupils who have participated in it. Probably the most famous scheme for devising educational objectives is the one associated with Benjamin Bloom and his colleagues who devised the so-called Taxonomy of Educational Objectives, which is adapted in table 8.

Table 7: Assessment — Functions and Characteristics

Purposes of Measurement

1 Placement in group
2 Diagnosis of difficulty
3 Assessment of performance
4 Prediction of performance
5 Evaluation of course

Assessment Programme Characteristics

1 Comprehensive — should relate to all areas in which progress should be made
2 Dynamic — should be responsive to changing school needs
3 Unobtrusive — should not interfere with the curriculum, but integral part of course
4 Practicable — should be realistic in relation to school context
5 Valid — the content should relate to course and needs of pupils
6 Reliable — should be consistent in quality and marking techniques

It has been said that the traditional form of written work assessment is concerned with memorization and precis-making, and that the main criteria of success are the maintenance of relevance and the ability to write fluently. This is still the basic form of procedure for assessment in the academic world of the humanities, but we need to look considerably further than simply the ability to recall elements of knowledge, which is very often all that is done by both objective questions and by structured questions. If we look at the two main

Table 8: Educational Objectives in Social Disciplines

Traditional form of written work assessment:

'Memorize
Summarize
Maintain relevance
Write fluently'

ASSESSMENT FEATURES BASED ON BLOOM'S TAXONOMY:

Cognitive Domain

Knowledge

(a)   Knowledge of *specific* information, terminology
(b)   Knowledge of methods of handling information; conventions, classification
(c)   Knowledge of principles, theories and structures

Comprehension

(a)   Translation — from one language form to another
(b)   Interpretation
(c)   Extrapolation

Application

Use of concepts in 'real world' situations

Analysis

(a)   Analysis of elements, for example distinguishing fact from hypothesis
(b)   Analysis of relationships — between concepts, events, features

Synthesis

Putting together elements to form a coordinated, coherent pattern or structure:

(a)   Skill in combining disparate ideas or facts
(b)   Production of an organized plan

Evaluation

Making informed value judgments on:

(a)   External 'close' evidence
(b)   External evidence by the standards of other cultures

Affective Domain

1   Sensitivity/awareness/consciousness
2   Responsiveness — willingness to accept participation and involvement
3   Development of ethical values (Kohlberg etc — see Lawton, D *et al* (1978) *Theory and Practice of Curriculum Studies*)
4   Organization of consistent values

areas explored by Bloom and his colleagues, they are the *cognitive domain* which is concerned with intellectual abilities, and the *affective domain* which is concerned more with the emotions and values. Bloom has established a hierarchy of cognitive skills, starting with 'knowledge', which at its lowest level is a recall of specific information and of terminology; and at its highest level, is 'evaluation' which is concerned with making value judgments on different forms of evidence. Obviously what we need to do for the much more demanding work offered by this sort of scheme is to make sure that the assessment procedures are not only comprehensive as far as we can make them, that is that they examine the development of a range of skills and informed values and attitudes, but that they make an assessment on the basis of not only whether children can recall particular items but whether they can use knowledge, whether they can analyze the sort of knowledge that they have presented to them, and whether they can interrelate the sorts of knowledge which they have acquired. This is suggested in the ranking order of the elements of Bloom's Taxonomy.

In this handbook it is suggested that each curriculum unit not only has its objectives and strategies clearly specified, but it is considered whether for any individual unit particular forms of assessment rather than general assessment procedures should be used. An example has been given to suggest that the study of material particularly related to the subject discipline, for example, economics, history or geography, may require rather different assessment procedures than those which will be common to all the units. It would be reasonable to expect that for each unit there is a pupil assessment sheet to record the progress that the pupil has made through this specific element of learning, and that on this assessment sheet it would be reasonable to specify the amount of effort and initiative used by the pupil, to consider the quality of the work, written, oral and practical, where this is appropriate, and to record any forms of 'hard-edge' assessment used.

In this way one might assume that at the end of the year, for each pupil there should be somewhere between eight and fifteen sheets which relate to the work of the pupil in all the curriculum units to which he or she has been 'exposed'. This should also markedly improve the writing of reports to parents, however often these are used. It is assumed here that the amount of energy expended on this will be well justified in the curriculum and homework-time given to the humanities, and it will also provide not only better report information for pupils than the conventional ones still used in many schools, but also for much more effective completion of internal school pupil records. It is not suggested that these pupil assessment forms be completed on a ratio of more than one for each unit — that would seem to me to be too demanding on teacher time and patience — nor is it suggested that the report be completed by the teacher without the pupil's knowledge. By far the most effective forms of pupil assessment, whatever particular procedures are used, are those where the teacher is communicating directly with the pupil, and, conveying to her why the assessment form presents this particular information or valuation. There should be an element of negotiation between teacher and pupil in the completion of the assessment form.

If we look at general objectives for the humanities, we are likely to select a number of factors such as the following: (the first is an abstract from some of the objectives defined by Professor Dennis Lawton in the BBC booklet (1977) *Middle Years at School*).

'Is she learning to distinguish evidence from supposition?'
'Is she learning about human control over the environment?'
'Is she experiencing comparisons between different societies?'
'Is she learning techniques of recording and presenting information?'
'Is she learning how to make deductions and judgments from a variety of forms of evidence, for example, films, books, fieldwork, artefacts and so on?'

These are only some of the learning objectives, but they are particularly significant ones in that we are not assessing knowledge recall, but the development of skill and understanding, and of practical techniques. If we look at what we might regard as a very basic minimum list of knowledge, skills and attitudes to be acquired in the two main contributory disciplines, geography and history in the early secondary years, then we might appear with a list something like this:

For history, the pupil should (a) know places, people, events in the locality; (b) know places, people and events in Britain in the past in order to understand the present; (c) know something about periods in the history of other countries and be able to put people in their 'national' context; (d) have experience of primary sources; (e) be able to make records in a variety of forms; (f) value resources used in the learning of history.

For geography, the pupil should (a) know major features of the local environment; (b) have techniques of contrasting and comparing small communities; (c) be able to record ideas in a variety of forms; (d) be able to identify features on maps and draw conclusions from them; (e) be able to use a variety of resources such as maps, books, photographs, films, (f) be able to give an adequate description of a location; (g) be able to identify some major features of world geography.

When we consider these cognitive and affective skills applied to the particular units that have been identified, we arrive at a need for a

Figure 25: Evaluating the Curriculum through Pupil(s) Progress

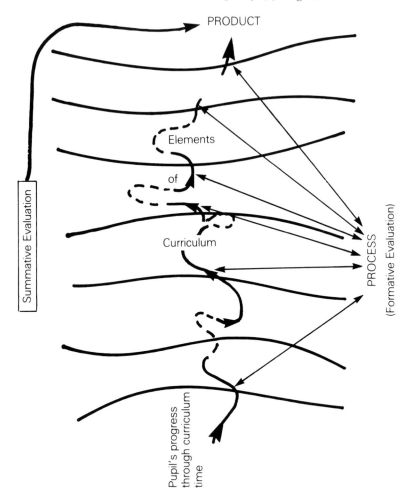

variety of assessment procedures. It is here that attention should be drawn to two different, although compatible, forms of assessment procedure. The first is described as *summative*, in that it is essentially concerned with the product of learning; that is, one makes a final judgment about pupil performance at the end of a course. This has certain limited advantages in that if the assessment, for instance, is to produce some sort of ranking order of individual performance amongst the members of the group, then this is done with a degree of facility if the objectives are relatively limited. On the other hand, because effective summative assessment would be long and arduous — that is it would take a very high proportion of the total time — it tends generally to be very ineffectual in the measurement of total pupil learning, unless, that is, it is accompanied by some sort of *formative* assessment. This is where we are measuring the encounters the pupil has had in developing understanding and skills during a course; the appropriate mode is continuous assessment, which is well developed by many 'practitioners' of CSE courses. The basic practice of continuous assessment is that the teacher is continually monitoring the progress of individual pupils, is modifying the course elements to relate to pupil needs, and is making a series of formative judgments as she 'goes along'. This seems to me a much more realistic way of looking at assessment, although undoubtedly it takes more effort and initiative on the part of the teacher and accounts for its very widespread adoption in schools; this is the form used in many 'progressive' schools rather than simply the assessment of pupil progress by testing the 'end product' of the knowledge acquired.

Objective questions tend to be concerned mainly with knowledge recall, although there is some element of analysis in a few questions, particularly of the 'assertion/reason' type. The most effective questions, however, are likely to be structured questions, in that here one can more efficiently test the skills and understanding that the pupils should have acquired through following the course. If one thinks of particular examples and applies these to the units, one could reasonably assess some of the knowledge and ideas that the pupils have acquired. The major advantage of the structured question is that the best examples of this can help to break down the curriculum into a number of sub-units. The most effective form of

Table 9: Written and Oral Assessment: Some Examples and Issues

Written Questions

(a) Objective
(b) Open-ended
(c) Structured

Objective Questions

(a) Matching/Classification
for example, people — eras

Julius Caesar	— Tudor
Mary Stuart	— Viking
Thomas Becket	— Industrial Revolution
Canute	— Roman
Sam Crompton	— Mediaeval

(b) True/False
for example, Circle 'T' if definite evidence to support.
Circle 'F' if no definite evidence to refute.
TF   (i)   The average Indian is poorer than the average American.
TF   (ii)   The French are happier than the English
TF   (iii)   Japan's exports of goods are worth more than those of Britain.

(c) Multiple — choice
for example, Stem + Key + Distractors
The main reason for Northampton's population growth during the last ten years is:
   (i)   The very high birth-rate.
   (ii) Many people coming in from the nearby countryside.
   (iii) Its development as an expanded town.
   (iv) The nearness of the M1 motorway.

(d) Multiple — completion
for example, Select A if 1, 2 and 3 are correct.
Select B if 1, 3 and 4 are correct.
Select C if 1, 2, 3 and 4 are correct.
Select D if 3 and 4 are correct.
British Prime Ministers since 1964 include:-
   1. Harold Wilson
   2. Winston Churchill
   3. Edward Heath
   4. James Callaghan

(e) Assertion/Reason
   (i)   Select which of the following statements is true and show if any statement is an explanation of another statement.
      (a) Corby is facing a crisis in its industrial future.
      (b) The iron ore in the nearby area has been worked out.
      (c) The steel-making capacity of Corby Works has been ended.
   (ii) For the following statements, indicate which ones are correct, and explain any connections between the statements.
      (a) The 'boat people' left Vietnam.
      (b) The Vietnam Government did not want them to leave the country.
      (c) The 'boat people' are mainly Chinese by origin.
      (d) The 'boat people' were not welcome in other Asian countries.

Open-Ended Questions

Attempts to overcome subjective marking
(a) Analytic mark scheme
(b) Standardization by sample
(c) Multiple impression marking

Structured Questions

Importance of:
(a) logical sequencing
(b) relation of questions and material
(c) balance of response needed

Oral Assessment

Fluency — use of vocal potential
Flow of ideas
Develop argument
Oral work related to project
Oral assessment of group discussions
(a) Value judgments
(b) Intellectual development
(c) Nature of evidence

Table 10: Assessment Procedures

APU – LANGUAGE PERFORMANCE

Reading Activities

1 Reading to gain overall impression of passage.
2 Reading to select information from different passages.
3 Reading to expand on given information.
4 Reading to follow sequence of instruction.
5 Reading to answer questions by direct reference.
6 Reading to detect implicit information.
7 Reading to detect bias and type of writing.
8 Reading for pleasure.

Writing for 15 Year Olds

1 Personal response to visual/aural stimuli.
2 Autobiographical, reflective narrative.
3 Fiction.
4 Objective account of process from pupil knowledge.
5 Persuasion on issue of pupils' own choice.
6 Account of problem solved or task performed.
7 Discussion of issue based on pupil evidence.
8 Discussion of issue on presented evidence.

structured question is where a particular stimulus is given. So, for example, if one is looking at a curriculum unit such as C16, which is concerned with motorway and airport location, one can study not only the development of attitudes and empathy in understanding the viewpoint of the various groups for and against the development of a motorway or an airport in a particular region or location, but one can use a great variety of stimulus material. A map of the area may be used with superimposed 'decibel zones', or a map which indicates land use in the area and the effect on land use created by the construction of a motorway or by an airport. One can examine photographs of an area 'before and after', and can consider statistical tabulations of expected population changes or employment opportunities offered.

It is by comparing the evidence on these issues in a test situation that one can effectively assess the progress of children. This progress, of course, is likely to be much more effectively assessed with some children if there is not a rigid, finite time limit on the assessment procedure. If one considers another unit such as B10, which is concerned with 'Invasion and succession in the pre-technical era' and which gives examples of either Saxons and Vikings or English and Normans, one can again use a range of map simulations, diagrams and information about the persons and graphs likely to be involved. The children are being asked to make assessments on the evidence provided, to draw from their knowledge of the period and to make deductions about the sort of developments which are likely to take place.

A number of examples are given of the 'forms' which can be used in objective questions; some of them have much more validity than others.

It is worth bearing in mind that virtually all the experts who have given much time to consider assessment procedures tend to come down to the three basic factors making for effective assessment: that is *comprehensiveness* — assessment procedures which closely match the curriculum objectives and the course elements of the curriculum; *validity*, which is the degree to which the test actually measures the objectives laid down, and may also have an element of prediction, in that it should suggest in performance how well the student will do at a later or more advanced stage; and *reliability* — the assessment technique used should not vary from time to time — (one of the major problems of providing adequate test material, in that there is a highly subjective element in most school-based assessment procedures).

In relation to the needs of humanities teachers, if we can see ways by which there can be consortia of schools combining in the design and production of curriculum units, then undoubtedly a body of expertise would be developed in the construction of assessment devices, so that it should be possible to gain an overall balance between the various modes and styles of assessment.[1] If assessment has considerable difficulties we should be aware of the even greater difficulties in making effective course evaluation. In the humanities there is the particular complication of the necessity to have a humanities course with an overall compatibility with school aims and objectives, so that when one makes an evaluation of a school in general by whatever means, whether formal or in terms of more intuitive judgments, one looks at the way that each curricular area reflects general school policy or diverges from it. Some of the complicated issues related to this are indicated in figure 25 and in the associated figure 26. I have deliberately emphasized two categories here as being relevant to our particular concern, the 'Curriculum system' and the 'Assessment system'.

One of the most controversial elements here is one of the items in the 'Assessment system' entitled 'Pupils' understanding of assessment procedures', and a related item from 'Curriculum system' entitled 'The curriculum satisfies pupil needs — evidence'. One of the most difficult tasks I have had to accomplish when discussing the humanities curriculum with secondary school teachers is to persuade many of them of the of the desirability of having feedback from the pupils on the content and relative degree of attractiveness of, or aversion from, the curriculum.

Figure 26: Sample sheet

ASSESSMENT	UNIT – D 8 AMERICAN WEST	GROUP 4 A.D.	WEEKS 26–29 (MARCH)	NAME SANDRA HILL
INPUT	READING — Penguin and Macdonald, *Wild West, Navaho, Colour Magazine, Historical Atlas*			
	AURAL/VISUAL TV — *End of American Frontier, How the West was Won, Soldier Blue* ('extra') (school) (adult)			
	TEACHER — Talk with OHP, simulation — railway pioneers			
OUTCOME	*Understanding of issues/empathy* — sees American view, sympathizes with horses, not cog. land issue.			
Use of sources	— *narrative reading good. Needs more use of maps, statistics. Follows films, uncritical. Not use photos well.*			
Presentation	— Good imaginative description *Waggon Trail*. Good pictures — railway building, Indian village. Map inaccurate, incomplete.			
Initiative	— Reads novel — *Smith Family in Rockies*. Unable develop Indian story.			
Other information — Sandra absent for two hours of 'lesson-time'. Extra work given with maps of USA, help with statistics.				

N.B. 1 The basic format is the same for all units, including the factors measured.
2 The pupil is responsible for completing most of the 'input' section as well as the 'titling'.
3 The 'outcome' section is completed by the teacher with the pupil present.

This is an example of a pupil assessment sheet that could be used for each unit with minor modifications. It emphasises the 'total experience' which the pupil receives on this theme and indicates 'outcome' on four dimensions selected to represent the diversity of 'measurement' of student work.

Figure 27: *Evaluating a School*

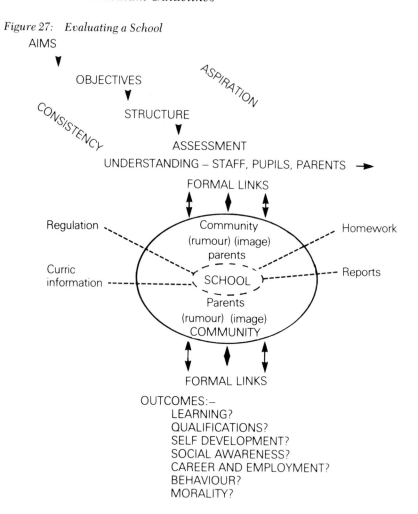

AIMS

OBJECTIVES   ASPIRATION

CONSISTENCY   STRUCTURE

ASSESSMENT

UNDERSTANDING – STAFF, PUPILS, PARENTS →

FORMAL LINKS

Regulation   Community   Homework
                    (rumour) (image)
                    parents

Curric
information   SCHOOL   Reports

Parents
(rumour) (image)
COMMUNITY

FORMAL LINKS

OUTCOMES:–
LEARNING?
QUALIFICATIONS?
SELF DEVELOPMENT?
SOCIAL AWARENESS?
CAREER AND EMPLOYMENT?
BEHAVIOUR?
MORALITY?

Reproduced are two question sheets which give an idea of the sort of things that have been asked in a number of schools. The sheets are called 'Subject perceptions' and 'Curriculum evaluation'. Both of them ask for a direct unrestricted pupil response on the parts of the curriculum which they like and which they dislike, and also their personal choices about some major elements in the hidden curriculum, so that some of the questions in 'Curriculum evaluation' are concerned with pupil response to the media. I would not suggest that this sort of pupil feedback form is used very often, but certainly it would provide an invaluable guide to teachers if it were used, perhaps once a year, in order to make an assessment of pupil response to the curriculum and of how effective is the understanding in depth of the subjects and disciplines.

Figure 28:   Evaluation by School Profile

'Profile' concerned with Organisation, Resources, Staff Development, Community Contacts, Pupil Welfare, Curriculum and Assessment.

Curriculum	*Assessment*
1 Adequate curriculum programmes.	1 System consonant with school aims.
2 Consonant with school aims.	2 Focus on individual progress.
3 Evidence of response to pupil needs.	3 Pupils and staff understand procedures.
4 Provision for special pupil needs.	4 Criterion and norm referencing.
5 Balance of curriculum choice in core and options — 'open system.'	5 Variety of techniques: — Formal, Continuous, Oral, Written, Resource using.
6 Pupils and staff know curriculum sequence, rationale.	6 Pupil response utilized.
7 Extra-curriculum provision response to pupil needs easpirations.	7 Course validation developed material appraised.
8 Curriculum links with feeder and successor schools.	8 Links with other schools, instits.
9 Staff opportunity for curriculum development, teaching innovation.	9 Creative, critical stance to examination bodies.
10	10 Continuous, varied non-academic pupil appraisal.
11	11

Table 11:   Curriculum Evaluation

Some Sentence Completions

1   During SUBJECT lessons my teacher wants me to . . . .
    because . . . .
2   My teacher says we have SUBJECT lessons so that . . . .
3   Learning SUBJECT will . . . .
4   SUBJECT helps me to . . . .
    because . . . .
5   If I had my way in SUBJECT we would stop . . . .
6   I like writing about . . . .
7   Talking is easier when . . . .
8   The sort of films I like are . . . .
9   The television programme I always watch is . . . .
    because . . . .
10 My favourite magazine is . . . .
    because . . . .
11 My favourite comic is . . . .
    because . . . .
12 The most interesting part of a newspaper is . . . .
13 We should have more time to . . . .
14 The things I would like to learn about that we are not taught in school are . . . . . .
    . . . .
    because . . . .
15 The sort of lessons I like best are . . . .
    because . . . .

Table 12:   Subject Perceptions

A   Complete the following sentences:
1   History is useful because . . . .
. . . .

2   Geography is useful because . . . .
. . . .

3   In history what I most like learning about . . . .
. . . .
but I am not interested in . . . .

4   In geography what I most like learning about . . . .
. . . .
but I am not interested in . . . .

5   I find geography difficult when . . . .
. . . .

6   I find history difficult when . . . .
. . . .

7   In geography and history we need to spend more time on . . . .
. . . .
. . . .

8   Economics is about . . . .
. . . .

9   Politics is about . . . .
. . . .

10   Sociology is about . . . .
. . . .

B   Write a description of the things you would like to study in these subjects . . . . . .
. . . .
. . . .
. . . .

I have set out on one page what I consider to be some of the basic questions which would need to be asked about any humanities curriculum in making a judgment about its effectiveness, but of course in the end one is faced with the need to evaluate the curriculum on a number of levels, apart from its consistency with overall policy. The levels which are most teasing to judge are those concerned with the outcomes of measuring pupil progress against curriculum validity. In other words if the staff are convinced that the content of the curriculum course is adequate and well balanced, but the pupils are failing to perform adequately in relation to the distribution of their abilities, what sort of lessons are to be learned? This takes us back to the fundamental diagram about 'Curriculum design', because here one may be looking at the structure of the course itself, at the relationship among the units, at the provision in the units for work matching all levels of pupil activity; or one may be looking at some very fundamental questions about whether the resources available relate closely enough to the course structure, or whether there is a balance of learning skills within each unit. These problems may seem to be very difficult to answer, but undoubtedly answers are provided by the experience of assessing the value of the units for the needs of the pupils and, above all, by the exchange of information and expertise amongst teachers in the same school, as well as amongst teachers in different schools.

We are now witnessing a great revival of interest in pupil profiling and school-and area-based certificates of achievement. Used wisely this should allow schools to make a much more just and effective appraisal of pupil performance and potential. Assessment in humanities on profile and certificate will be an effective discipline in rethinking some of our objectives in this area of the curriculum when we redefine it in terms of the need to participate in a changing adult society. Relevant to this document is the invaluable pupil diary that was developed in a number of primary schools and which was introduced into a small number of secondary comprehensive schools, particularly in earlier years. Most of us will know of the pupil work diary but, for those who do not, briefly it consisted of a diary in which the pupil recorded not only day-to-day school- and home-work, including reasons for absence or particularly good performance or bad performance, but where the pupil was encouraged to make a very honest appraisal of the elements of the curriculum by stating whether they enjoyed the work or found the work difficult. In other words, the pupil's diary related closely to the pupil curriculum evaluation sheets. Certainly this diary would be particularly useful as applied to a unit-based humanities curriculum, in that it would then be possible for teachers to get more that an intuition about the relative success of a unit, and because the unit system is relatively so easy to change, it would allow for continuous modification and alteration as the units were used over a period of time.

The Assessment of Gifted Children and Diagnosis of their Needs

The general assumption made about the needs of gifted children in following a scheme of work is that there should be a change in the quality of the work. These children should be provided with more difficult material and be expected to work at a much higher level of abstraction. In general the objective is that the children should acquire accelerated learning skills, which are then applied to more difficult problems than is the general age cohort.

In the assessment and identification of the attributes of gifted-ness one should look for the following features.

First of all, these children will show accurate observation and classification of the elements of knowledge.

Secondly, gifted children exhibit precision and certainty in the selection of the salient features of an issue or a problem or process, so that the children show their ability to go straight to the essentials of a matter and to reject the surrounding 'clutter'.

Thirdly, these children are generally able to hypothesize about patterns, to discover uniqueness and to make predictions and extrapolations.

Fourthly, they will usually adopt a critical stance towards the sources of information, including the textbooks and, more dauntingly, their teachers.

Fifthly, if one takes the Liam Hudson typology of convergent and divergent thinkers, a considerable number of gifted children are likely to be at the 'creative' rather than at the 'conforming' pole. There has been considerable doubt about the correlation between creativity and measured intelligence, but, leaving these issues aside, one should look in gifted children for the lateral thinker, for the child who questions conventional assumptions and shows, I suppose, one of the few distinguishing marks of both genius and madness — that is, the pupils who are 'out of their own time and place'.

Sixthly, as a corollary of the previous feature of lateral thinking, gifted children are likely to deviate considerably from teacher expectations. 'If she does not keep pace with her companions, perhaps it is because she hears the music of a different drummer'. Such children are not likely to perform well on a lot of the standard assessment procedures, in that either they will instinctively or intuitively reject a lot of the test material as irrelevant, or their own assumptions will have projected beyond the assumptions of the teachers in whose charge they are lodged.

It is particularly important that gifted children are given the opportunity to meet with other gifted children and adults. Again one of the characteristics of children with exceptional giftedness is that some of the normal segregation patterns based on age and status seem to them, as they probably are, irrelevant. For the characteristics of gifted children and their curriculum needs, it is useful to consult two basic booklets, one published for the Department of Education and Science, as a result of Her Majesty's Inspectorate investigations, called *Gifted Children and Their Education* and another, more recent DES publication, also from Her Majesty's Inspectorate, (1978) *Gifted Children in Middle and Secondary Comprehensive Schools*.

When one looks at the sorts of development in assessment procedures which would be needed to monitor the progress of gifted children, one arrives at a variety of injunctions rather than achievements. Here are some examples:

1   They should be particularly encouraged to question textbook interpretations and look for other explanations than those given by textbook authors, and to consider the justifications which the authors of textbooks produce.

2   In the field of geography, much of the assessment of gifted-

Table 13: Some Humanities Evaluations

1 Does course allow entry of concepts/ideas from other disciplines?
2 Is there a conscious attempt to examine bias?
3 Does the humanities curriculum respond to and influence other curricular areas?
4 Is there variation in
   (a) teaching styles?
   (b) course material?
   (c) assessment modes?
5 What determines the structure of the course — chronology, topography, concepts, —?
6 How far does the course tackle fundamental questions about human behaviour?
7 How much of the work is orientated towards hypothetico-deductive methods applied to evidence?
8 What procedures exist for modifying the course by feedback from evaluation and pupil assessment?
9 What process operates to select geographical content in order to develop conceptual understanding?
10 What process operates to select historical content to illustrate fundamental social behavioural experiences?
11 How effectively are the interdisciplinary and the unidisciplinary elements identified?
12 Does the course programme relate to the understanding of major contemporary issues?
13 How does the course develop the making of value judgments?
14 Does the course maintain a balance between the implications of possibilism and determinism?
15 How does course develop encounters with 'high' culture and popular culture?
16 Are creative, divergent thinking processes fostered?

ness should look at the role of geographers in planning the environment, so gifted children should be able to examine a variety of viewpoints concerning environmental change and location factors for various man-made artefacts, whether hypermarkets or factories or 'amusement institutions'. Gifted children should certainly show some talent in producing simulations which will extend and amplify issues about planning and modifying the human environment. Another area where gifted children should be able to make a particularly useful contribution is in considering the problems of alternative intermediate technology in answering some basic human problems about the provision of energy in an over-crowded planet, of new ways of providing for housing and transport needs, and so on. It is partially for this reason that I have suggested a number of units in Phase Four concerned with (in American terminology) 'Futurology', simply because so much of science fiction is an effective 'trigger' for the consideration of these issues.

3 In history, a lot of the work that should tax the minds of the

gifted is concerned with alternative futures. The idea of alternative futures is perhaps particularly well expressed in a considerable amount of fiction. Memorable for me is James Thurber's early essay on the ending of the American Civil War entitled 'If Grant had been Drinking at Appomattox'.

Similarly William Golding has written, many years ago, a play exploring the situation where an eccentric scientist presents to a decadent Roman emperor the secrets of printing, gunpowder and the steam engine; the inventions are derided or used for trivial personal amusement.

Gifted children, if given the right sort of stimulus, should prove themselves adept at developing a critical awareness of the context of the media. Skills include the ability to examine printed and audio-visual material with the object of investigating authorship, intended readership, match of illustrations and text, and to pose sych fundamental questions as 'Which people or events are consciously or unconsciously rendered invisible in this account?'

It is through the lives of people out of their own times that gifted children can gain great imaginative insights. The sort of people who are likely to inspire and concern children with this diversity of talent or even with a singleness of talent developed to a great extent, are people like Leonardo da Vinci, Thomas Edison or Madame Curie.

In the social sciences there should be no difficulty in providing gifted children with a great range of interesting developments on which to focus their understanding. Random examples would be to consider the development of religious belief systems through something like the 'Cargo Cults of Micronesia' or to look at the situation envisaged by some anthropologists in fictional form. A good example here would be the novel *Earth Abides* by George Stewart, which envisages the elimination of a large part of the human population by plague and a re-working of the themes of Frazer's *Golden Bough*.

The major contribution that gifted children can make to us is their ability to project beyond the immediate situation, and it is from gifted children that we could learn a considerable amount about improvements in course design and in diagnosing and rewarding the abilities of the lateral thinking and the divergent.

Note

1   There are a number of excellent handbooks on assessment procedures, but outstanding for our purposes is the handbook by Henry Macintosh (1976) in the Canterbury Study Book series. *Assessing Attainment in the Classroom* published by Hodder and Stoughton.

Chapter 11

Some Important Issues

Underlying all discussion of curriculum planning is the crucial issue of whether humanities should be taught in an interdisciplinary way or taught as single subjects such as history, geography and social studies. This issue seems to have generated more heat than light, in that the discussion about single subjects or an interdisciplinary curriculum in the middle years, has now raged furiously for about a decade. There are good reasons for avoiding both extreme positions; on the one hand there are those schools which treat history, geography, social studies and religious studies as completely separate subjects, and where the teachers of single subjects maintain a reluctance to be concerned with the other subjects, and on the other hand, there are those schools where it is difficult to identify the contributory disciplines in inter-disciplinary schemes. The most effective schemes are those which consciously draw on the disciplines for their structure and suste-nance. If one looks at the reasons for the interdisciplinary studies given by proponents of this system in the accompanying 'list' (table 14), I think most of us would agree that all of these are valid reasons, but they are valid in the sense that they can only be effective with staff who are quite aware of not only the commonality of the humanities disciplines, but who are also aware of the disciplines' unique contributions. Each of the humanities subjects has a particular way of interpreting the world by using particular skills and ideas which form its conceptual structure but, more importantly perhaps, they have common concerns with the explanation and understanding of human social behaviour. 'Interdisciplinarity' has 'taken on' a heavy additional load, in that very often it has been associated with a degree of progressivism in education which has found its main base in child-centred learning, and interdisciplinarity is usually, although not universally, associated with mixed-ability teaching groups.

Pupils in schools and students in higher education, both stress one particularly important feature of the ways in which they learn; that is their strongly expressed wish for a variety of learning styles. One of the consequences of the move towards resource-based

Table 14:   Alleged Reasons for Interdisciplinary Studies

1   To explore themes, areas and problems, which lie outside conventional subject boundaries.
2   To use subject skills as tools for the solution of problems that extend beyond conventional subject boundaries.
3   To increase the individual pupil's power to decide, and to pursue, his own learning paths.
4   To allow gifted children the opportunity to explore areas of work which might otherwise be denied them.
5   To allow staff to use to their full potential the wide range of skills which might happen to be outside their own subjects.
6   To explore relationships between subjects.
7   To improve definition of subjects by understanding common concerns and distinctive attributes.

Table 15:   'Collection' and 'Integrated' Life Styles

Dimension	from (collection codes)	to (integrated codes)
Curriculum content	Separate subjects	Interdisciplinary
Pedagogy	Instruction	Enquiry activities
Organization of teaching/learning	Rigid timetabling	Flexible timetabling
Pupil grouping	Homogenous	Heterogeneous
Pupil choice	Limited	Extensive
Assessment	Single code	Multiple codes
Basis of pupil control	Position in hierarchy	Personal relations
Teacher roles	Independent	Interdependent

(from an essay by Professor Eric Hoyle)

learning in the 1970s was a consideration of a variety of resources by which children could learn, and particular applications in their use, on the assumption that all human beings vary in the way they react to stimuli. There is no reason to suppose that children's basic learning process in school will be different essentially from those outside the school in spite of the school's regulations and fixed definitions. Many schools have mixed ability groups, certainly until the age of 13, and some of them retain mixed-ability groups in most parts of the curriculum until the age of 16. In practice, as is generally recognized, all groups are mixed-ability groups, or mixed-motivation groups, or mixed-privilege groups. Although mixed-ability teaching in the humanities has been particularly associated with interdisciplinarity, there is no necessary relationship any more than there is a necessary relationship with the need to provide a variety of learning styles where there is a wide range of intelligence and motivation.

However, there are certain particular implications about the development of a resource-based learning system which is combined with a wide range of ability in particular classrooms. Especially important is the time-tabling of humanities lessons, so there are particular problems about children with a wide range of ability and motivation, and the provision of a variety of resources where this is combined with a number of lessons of a duration of thirty minutes or less. Although the unit system of planning removes some of the difficulties inherent in this situation, one can assume that the thirty-minute lesson, preceded and followed by lessons of quite different types and in different curricular areas, is incompatible with certain types of learning. Nevertheless, the thirty-minute lesson can be used effectively: for example, the short exposition by the teacher, particularly of key ideas for the Unit to be developed, of for individual work or group work that is a continuation of work already initiated during a longer teaching period.

One must stress in mixed-ability groups, as indeed it should be stressed in all groups, the importance of practical work. A myth grew up in some educational quarters during the last decade that it was impossible to give formal teacher-centred lessons to mixed-ability groups. There seems to be little evidence that this is so in practice, but that it is necessary for teachers to mix formal instructions, which they may believe is the most effective method of inducting certain ideas, with a variety of other learning modes. Each unit should be planned with the assumption that there would be a variety of appropriate learning styles, that is of mixing some teacher expositions and group work with some individual work. It is in the group work particularly that opportunity should be made for some of the time for the fast-learners to work together, particularly under the stimulus of more demanding work than the rest of the group get, and also to give some special help needed for the slow-learners. The specific forms of help for slow-learning pupils will depend on the mix of direct teacher-guidance as well as carefully-planned work cards or pupil guidelines.

As it will be desirable for all the teachers in the team to develop their specialist areas of knowledge as well as general competence across the humanities, it would be particularly desirable that certain members of humanities teams developed close links with other major curricular areas. It would certainly be desirable in the era of falling secondary rolls for the majority of teachers in humanities to also have some experience of teaching English or mathematics at a relatively limited level. Falling rolls will also exacerbate the problem of late entrants into the humanities. This is a situation that has always needed to be recognized, but there will be more people in the late 1980s and 1990s who are expected to teach humanities subjects where they either have a vestigial knowledge or perhaps a detailed subject knowledge but dating from the past; hence their image of the subject matter will be not of the present but of some past era in the evolution of the structure and assumptions of particular subjects.

The contraction of the number of pupils in the upper secondary years will bring with it a reconsideration of the relationships in the core curriculum of the fourth and the fifth years and the options schemes, which was a mode that become dominant in a large majority of secondary schools during the 1960s and 1970s. It seems likely now that many schools will adopt a humanities core in the fourth and fifth years, although many of them will keep history and geography, and perhaps other subjects, in the options scheme. Strong influences on the content and criteria of the humanities curriculum in the fourth and fifth years will be such schemes as the Joint Matriculation Board Humanities 'O' level and its 'CSE compatible' courses, and also the sorts of courses developed under the Modern Studies 'umbrella' in Scotland.

These schemes are likely to focus on social and political issues in the modern world within the context of what is increasingly termed 'the emerging present'[1]. This phrase is used to relate to the time-consciousness of people living in the present, where the present is conceived of as a moving line which encompasses those major events within about the last 100 years, with a projection of probable alternative futures within the next fifty years. The modular system should be sufficiently flexible to accommodate teaching about current controversial issues and the systems in which they are embedded.

It is particularly important that people are able to make effective value judgments about such issues as nuclear war, animal welfare, and inequality between the sexes, as all these issues have particularly important implications in the humanities.

There are already strong indications of gender differences in subject popularity as between the humanities and the natural sciences at 'A' level, and increasingly at 'O' level and CSE. Limited research has suggested that many boys are more interested in technology, and very often violence, whereas many girls of the same age — that is in the secondary years — are more likely to be interested in human relationships and more sensitive moral issues. This creates problems not only for the content of the humanities programme, but also for the type of teaching resources used. The fact that many boys appear to be more interested in the technical and mathematical aspects of physical geography, and in recent or con-temporary violent conflict, whereas girls may prefer the more humanistic geography and, in some cases, may have a strong liking for the more romantic and exotic in history may be largely attributable to the differences in the expectations of their roles in society. These tendencies should be matched by work which stresses the importance of individuals and which encourages a diversity of perspectives and interpretations of human behaviour.

It may be useful when studying an issue about political development to emphasize contrasting perceptions so that the boys may be able to give a more technocratic view and the girls a more sensitive appraisal of the personal and moral issues. This is certainly not to suggest that the humanities programme should set out to recognize or over-emphasize gender differences; the policy should be to retain them by treating boys and girls as individuals, many of whom may have something to contribute to the general understanding of these controversial issues.

One of the most important elements in curriculum planning in humanities is the further development of language and the necessary components of the language programme in learning about human behaviour. It is commonplace that too much of the language in schools tends to be transactional: that is its concern with information giving and receiving and very seldom is it expressive or poetic in its content or mode. The most effective learning of the use of language is by discussion, in that it is only by discussion that children learn to reorganize and reorientate the knowledge that they are acquiring. The sort of involvement that is necessary can only be developed by more issue-based learning and more emphasis on a variety of styles of presentation. Hence the importance that has been stressed in an earlier chapter of the use of simulations and role-plays. For students to engage in discussion that will enable them to express themselves more articulately and persuasively they need to be 'empathic insiders'. The questions that are likely to elucidate this particular form of linguistic behaviour are questions that open up discussions rather than close them down. The type of questions that are most useful are 'What would you do in this situation?' or 'What would happen if?', or 'How would you persuade these other people to alter their opinions or behaviour?' or 'How would you clarify these issues to yourself?' (by writing a diary of events, for example).

Students are likely to produce their most effective work when they are given the challenge of producing material to present to a variety of audiences, particularly if they can use equipment such as overhead projectors, slides and cassettes.

In this case the discipline of structuring their own learning and presenting it in a variety of forms for a variety of audiences is likely to be the greatest stimulus to the development of the imagination and its articulation. In this process pupils can learn to shape their thoughts in different ways according to different objectives, and to make with others a more thorough exploration of ideas and their consequences. Many projects that are conspicuously successful have something in common with the preparation of drama or the preparation of film or radio programmes. Even then, the continuing guidance and monitoring of the teacher is essential, particularly to guide pupils into the modification of their own ideas and by exploring aspects of a particular problem or development that may not be immediately observable. This to a certain extent may take the form of a structuring of enquiry. It is often seen at its best in classes in primary schools which are environmentally focussed and where the children are taught to explore through all the senses, so that smell and touch, and even taste, are as important as listening and observing.

There are particular problems about the acquisition of an appropriate vocabulary in the humanities, and there are dangers certainly in history and sociology and politics of terms being unconsciously used by teachers and lecturers in a way that presupposes a dense cluster of ideas and associations that the teacher may have but which the pupils are unlikely to possess. If one thinks of terms such as 'feudal', 'totalitarian', 'network', 'political party' and 'industrial location', all of these have associations in depth and are used by people already within the disciplinary area with a wide association of meanings and contexts. There should be a developing glossary of terms used for each of the units but the only way that these terms can be understood is by the general teaching of ideas and concepts; that is by a progressive spiral curriculum that uses each of these terms in a more sophisticated, elaborated way as the learning of the pupils increases. The particular problems about the use of the specialist terms in the humanities is twofold; there are certain terms which have a general meaning in everyday discourse but have a specialist meaning for the historian, geographer and sociologist, and there are other terms that really encapsulate 'embedded concepts' from these disciplinary bases. This indicates that there should be a planned introduction and definition-building of many of the terms that continue to be important throughout the learning of the humanities and the social sciences. Associated with these are terms that are particularly important because they are concerned with essential features of the humanities such as causation, contrast, and location in time and space. It is these words that are used across the curriculum that need particular attention in developing in students an effective, fluent written style and conceptual understanding.

The implementation of the interdisciplinary unit system in schools which have had conventional subject separation, with lesson-by-lesson schemes of work, is usually best achieved by introducing units over quite a long period of time. If one thought of twelve units in a particular year as being a desirable number, it would be wise to assume that the most that could be effectively introduced in the first year would be about half of that. Before the curriculum in a particular year can be changed to the unit system it is necessary to make an analysis of the existing curriculum, particularly by identifying the concepts implicit in the themes taught. Some schemes of work may show an over-concentration of the political and the military in history, so that children get an 'overdose' of themes concerned with military conflict and monarchical power. Similarly in geography there are a few schools where there is an over-concentration on physical geography and on the study of rural, pastoral and primitive societies rather than on modern 'technological' society. Other biases may be shown in an over-emphasis on local work at the expense of wider ranging studies. The critical factor here is not so much the content but whether children are getting an exaggeration of one type of concept or experience at the expense of many other necessary learning concepts and experiences.

Related to this issue is another about how permanent a scheme should be. One of the advantages of a humanities curriculum which is based on skills, ideas and experiences, is that the units can be changed with relative frequency although presumably some of the subject matter of some of the units has sufficient validity to be used year after year. However, as the objective is understanding in depth — that is, the structure is based on the understanding of fundamental human experiences by using concepts and skills — then the units can be changed relatively often. This should go some way to alleviate the boredom for the teacher that can come with teaching the same subject matter year after year. The conceptual structure of the scheme should facilitate the exchange of units from one school to another, so that the school which, for instance, has considered the theme of 'invasion and succession' in history, or the theme of urbanization in geography, by using particular materials for a number of years, may well wish to teach the same concepts and experiences but to change the subject matter.

An effective humanities curriculum answers two central human needs if it is effectively designed and learned. The first need is that of giving children 'roots'; the humanities curriculum should help children to achieve a sense of personal and social identity in the same way that other major curricular areas can do. The humanities curriculum is essentially concerned with social relationships in time and place, so that children should learn where their families and their communities have 'originated' and how they relate to other individuals and communities at the present time. The second main objective of the humanities curriculum is to prepare children for 'changing destinations'. This is meant in a literal and also in a more metaphorical sense. Literally we may expect most of the present school population to change occupations and residence many times in their lives, unless the majority of social observers and prognosticators are completely wrong. So the humanities curriculum should have an emphasis on how communities have coped with change in the past, and should give strong indications of the likely changes that these children will encounter in their own lifetimes. Hence the importance of one of the basic English exercises: 'Write your own autobiography from the age of 50, or the age of 40, or the age of 70'.

Some American historians have suggested that from the perspective of another hundred years ahead the fundamental change in human experience may not be seen as the first Industrial Revolution, which has been cited by many historians as of equal human significance as, for instance, the discovery of fire or the development of a settled farming system. This group of historians and social scientists has suggested that the fundamental change in human history is now upon us: the change to a system where advanced technology has reached a stage where it can be virtually self-sustaining. A fundamental purpose of the humanities curriculum must be to give children the personal security to meet a variety of major social, economic and political changes, to help them to make a critical evaluative appraisal of the changes that take place, and to see themselves as participants in the process of change.

The deliberate use of material from the popular media, whether that of children's comics or the deliberate reference to, and the use of, adult television programmes, should give opportunities for an understanding of the importance of language, spoken and written, in the presentation of reality as well as in the presentation of opinion. It is from a conscious breaking down of some of the barriers between the formal curriculum and the hidden curriculum that some of the most inspiring and rewarding work can develop.

Note

1   See the publication by Slaughter, R A *Futures Education*, Centre for Peace Studies, St Martin's College, Lancaster

Appendix A

Schools Council Projects for the Middle Years

The Integrated Studies Project: this has long been completed although a lot of the material that was produced is of good quality and relates well to a number of the main units which I have suggested. Unhappily, some of the material that was produced was difficult to resource in schools and probably was too far away from the perceptions of what humanities was about when it was first published. I would advise people interested in this to contact the Oxford University Press directly.

The second project is the *Environmental Studies Project* with a clientele in the age range 5–13. This was also a project associated with the early years of the Schools Council and concentrated in producing teacher material which is quoted in the bibliography and referred to in the text. Two particular books, *Starting with Maps* and *Starting with Rocks*, have much to commend them.

Thirdly, the *History, Geography and Social Science Project*, more familarly known now as 'Time, Place and Society', was devised in the University of Liverpool Institute of Education in the early 1970s. The philosophy of Time, Place and Society is very close to the one that I have tried to promote in the handbook: that is, it assumes a considerable amount of teacher development, it conceives objectives as roads to travel rather than destinations to be achieved, and it is focussed on the development of a range of intellectual, social and physical skills as well as the development of interests, attitudes and values. Its basic curriculum structure is founded on seven key concepts: communication, power, values and beliefs, conflict and consensus (these concepts are concerned with social processes), and another three concepts which are concerned with the analysis of society: that is similarity and difference, continuity and change, and causes and consequences. Of particular use is the main project handbook which I have already referred to, *Curriculum Planning*, and particularly useful for comparison with the themes that I have tentatively suggested is the small handbook *Themes in Outline*. Amongst the themes selected are those relating to families, local

Table 16: Schools Council Project: Time, Place and Society

Suggested Objectives

A Reference Skills

A pupil who has developed reference skills CAN
(a) Use an index.
Use content headings as guides to the required material.
(b) Use the main kinds of reference books (junior encylopaedias etc) quickly and accurately.
Select an appropriate reference book for the purpose required.

B Physical Skills

A pupil who has developed physical skills CAN
(a) Operate a slide viewer.
(b) Operate a film strip projector.
(c) Operate a tape recorder.
(d) Operate a record player.

C Communication Skills

A pupil who has developed these skills CAN
(a) Provide accurate and legible diagrams to back his work.
(b) Set out a diagram clearly.
(c) Draw an accurate sketch map.
(d) Write a short narrative which is organized coherently.
(e) Present an argument logically, whether orally or in writing.
(f) Use body and speech to convey the essence of a character he or she is portraying.

D Comprehension Skills

A pupil who has developed these skills CAN
(a) Give the essence of a piece of material he has read (for example, 'According to this book they were very poor in those days').
(b) Can describe the main features of a piece of evidence (for example, 'Well, they went to school without breakfast, or without coats even in winter').

E Skills Related to Values and Empathy

A pupil who has developed these skills CAN
(a) Identify values on which human actions are based (for example, 'They didn't believe in that in those days').
(b) Recognize that holding certain values can determine actions (for example, 'They believed Sunday was a holy day so the children weren't allowed to play').
(c) Identify the extent of choice available to a person in a given situation (for example, 'You had to stay in your job. If you left you probably wouldn't get another').
(d) Understand some ideas from a 'culture' different from his own (for example, belief in Empire).
(e) Describe an incident with evidence of involvement (for example, a lesson in a Board School).
(f) Identify with a character under study so as to be able to declare the character's

viewpoint on a particular problem (for example, a person in the nineteenth century faced with the prospect of going into the workhouse).

(g)   Represent in dramatic form a character from another period (for example, a child from 1900).

F   Translation Skills

A pupil who has developed these skills CAN

(a)   Present verbal material in dramatic form (for example, make a play from log book extracts).

(b)   Present verbal material in the form of a graph
                              model
                              diagram
                              map

(c)   Describe the features of a picture or map accurately.

(d)   Turn information received in factual form into a narrative.

G   Reasoning Skills

A pupil who has developed these skills CAN

(a)   Make inferences from a piece of evidence — a document, picture, etc. (for example, 'Well, they had no boots so . . .').

(b)   Put a proposition to fill a gap in evidence (for example, 'I think they'd probably . . .').

(c)   Frame a hypothesis (for example, 'I think they did it because . . .').

(d)   Can back up a conclusion with appropriate evidence (for example, 'I think they weren't happy because you can't be happy when you're hungry, can you?').

(e)   Can evaluate a piece of evidence from the point of view of bias, etc. (for example, 'Yes, but he was only a boy then. Perhaps he doesn't remember very well').

community, leisure interests, industry, education, conflict, issues. Some of the material from the *Time, Place and Society Project* is available from the School Curriculum Development Committee.

Appendix B

Broadcast Resources

Although many schools make extensive use of live and recorded television and radio programmes, it may be useful for school staff to collectively review all recent programmes in order to appraise the variety of provision that is made. Both BBC and IBA have produced outstanding programme series and to accompany these programmes have produced a variety of pupil and teacher resources. It may be worth approaching other schools and institutions to find out if any of these materials are still available. Outstanding amongst them were series such as *Meeting our Needs* and *Exploration Man*, both produced by independent television companies.

FOR SCHOOL COMPLETION:
Television and radio programmes relevant to humanities modules.

Appendix C

Maps and Time-Lines

For the successful implementation of the study scheme, maps will need to be provided on a variety of scales; they are a basic artefact. Attached to this document you will see some excerpts from the Schools Council publication *Understanding Maps* which gives a useful taxonomy of a range of mapping and map-using skills. Important in this is the choice of media; that is, whether to have maps in the form of conventional wall-maps, or in the form of 35mm slides or overhead projector slides. Whatever the presentation medium, the recommended stock by way of a basic provision would have many items in the list. Important in this is the matter of the scale of the map used, the form of area presentation, and the subject matter. One of the major defects of many published maps is that too much information is presented on one base. It is far more useful to have a base map which gives only skeletal information that is basic — 'physical geography' for example — and on this to use a number of overlays in whatever form to suggest the coordination and interrelationships of natural and man-made features.

Basic List

1 (a) 1:1250 Ordnance Survey maps of the vicinity of the school or of the catchment area, and also of at least part of the town centre.
   (b) 1:2500 Ordnance Survey maps of sections of the local area.
   (c) 1:1000 Ordnance Survey maps of the entire local urban area.
   (d) 1:25000 Ordnance Survey maps of local areas.
   (e) 1:50000 Ordnance Survey map of local area and contrasted areas.
   (f) 1:63360 Ordnance Survey Geological Map.
   (g) 1:250000 Ordnance Survey Map.

Figure 29

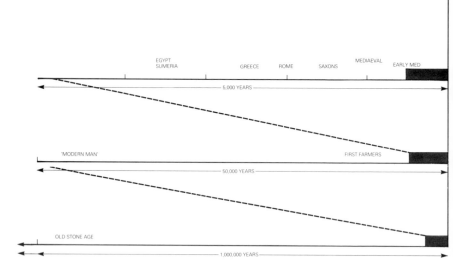

2 Wall maps available from a number of firms, for example, G Philip, Bartholomew. A recommended minimum stock would be physical and political maps of:
   (a) The British Isles.
   (b) Main continental areas (see Philip's *Comparative Wall Atlas*).
   (c) The world — showing relief climate, vegetation, population density.
3 A relief globe: a minimum size would need to be 45cm diameter.
4 Other maps:
   (a) Historical maps, for example, of County, First Edition Ordnance Survey maps.
   (b) Land use maps, for example, the Second Land Utilization Survey Map (not all local areas are available but other similar areas have been mapped).
   (c) Local Authority maps, for example, those available from County Planning Departments and from Development Corporations.
   (d) A number of commercial maps available showing particular industrial or commercial features.
   (e) Small set of Bartholomew's maps on the scale of 1:100,000.
5 Atlases
   In general the one type of atlas to be avoided for school

Figure 30

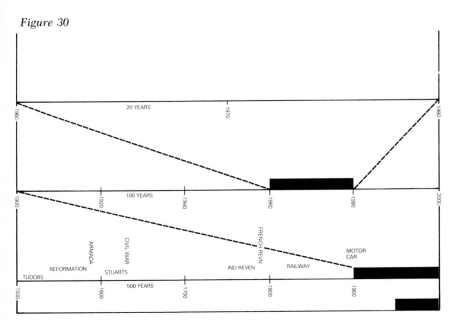

purchase, although not necessarily for pupil purchase, is the small format paperback which generally tries to present far too much information on far too small a page. A number of these paperback atlases are published by firms such as Penguin, Collins, and Chambers; they would be useful ancillaries but not effective atlases for school use.

(a) Atlases for the library, both geographical and historical: there are a number of outstandingly good publications available at comparatively low prices and the catalogues of the major firms such as Philip, Oxford, Collins, Longman, Bartholomew, should be consulted. An outstanding recent publication are Kidron and Segal's *State of the World Atlas* (Pan Reference), and the *Gala Atlas of Planet Measurement*, (Pan Reference).

(b) Student atlases: Some of the possible atlases would be the following:
The modern School Atlas (Philip's)
Atlas Four (Collins-Longman)
Atlas of Modern History (Philip)
Oxford School Atlas (Oxford University Press)
Atlas of the Environment (Bartholomew)
Intermediate Historical Atlas (Philip)
Nelson School Atlas

Time Charts

The most effective time charts are produced by teachers and students on a variety of scales, for example, wall charts on cartridge paper, wall charts produced on cartridge paper and then photographed on 35mm colour film, or wall charts on OHP slides — which is probably the most effective form. The recommended scales of the time charts are those based on the Oxford University Press publication, *The Unfolding Past*.

OHP recommendations are based on overlays on a 10" chronological scale:

1 1 million years
2 50,000 years
3 5000 years
4 500 years
5 100 years
6 20 years

All these scales end in the year 2000, except the last one, and some indication of their interrelationship is shown as presented on OHP slides and 'overlays' in a diagram in the text.

Appendix D

Objectives at Thirteen Years
(Abstracted from the Schools Council
Publication *Understanding Maps*)

The following objectives were formulated as a result of discussions by a teachers' working group at the Purbeck Teachers Centre. They are suggested as being appropriate mapping skills and concepts to work towards rather than a list of pupil standards to be attained by everyone. Children develop at different rates; what one child has attained, another may have only just started to understand.

General Geographical Skills Related to Mapping

By the age of thirteen years, children should normally be able to:

1 Find information from maps, photographs.
2 Use maps as a means of communication.
3 Organize information to be clearly displayed on maps.
4 Draw sketch maps and field sketches to show information.
5 Record information using a classification system as in graphs or maps.
6 Use maps as investigatory tools.
7 Study maps as sources of interest as well as information.

Specific Mapping Skills

By the age of thirteen years, children should normally be able to:

1 Draw maps based on perception, measurement, or representation (sketch).
2 Draw from perception a labelled map of a small well known area showing estimated distances and directions.
3 Compare the perception map with a large scale plan of the vicinity.

4   Develop a personal set of symbols and corresponding key for maps and plans they have designed themselves.

5   Build up a creative graphicacy, for example, maps of 'my island' or 'my secret valley'.

6   Recognize direction and be able to orient a map.

7   Draw diagrams of cardinal points of the campass.

8   Find directions and bearings using a Silva compass.

9   Orient a map using a Silva compass.

10   Describe a route from a map using directions and estimated distances.

11   Follow a route using a map and directions.

12   Identify, draw and label symbols used on the 1:25000 or 1:50000 Ordnance Survey Maps.

13   Abstract information represented by the larger conventional signs.

14   Compile a key to illustrate information shown on a map.

15   Use coordinates to find places on maps; for example, by grid references, latitude and longitude.

16   Use grid references of given locations.

17   Plot information on plans.

18   Measure the straight line distance between two points correct to the nearest mile or kilometre.

19   Measure distances along winding routes with a tolerance of half-a-mile or kilometre.

20   Estimate distances on a map.

21   Recognize contour patterns of valleys, spurs, plateaux and ridges.

22   State elementary relationships between physical features and communications.

23   Draw elementary cross sections.

24   Describe the nature of slopes — steep, gentle, concave, convex.

25   Compute an average gradient between fixed points.

26   Describe a scene with the combined evidence of oblique photographs and map.

Selective Bibliography

This is a restricted bibliography: it will be found most useful in citing books which give insights into the main issues. It is very selective. Further detailed information will be found in the bibliographies of the books which are cited. The most important omissions are those which refer to materials published mainly for student use or which are an integral part of such publications as Schools Council Projects. I should particularly emphasize the usefulness and the quality of the handbooks from the Schools Council History 13–16 Project, the Avery Hill Geography Project, the 14–18 Geography Project, and the 16–19 Geography Project.

Many other projects, series and individual texts and films exemplify the approaches suggested in this handbook; it is not feasible to list them here but to simply commend the reader to the resources held in many Institutes and Departments of Education in universities and colleges. Many of these institutions publish particularly useful journals and occasional papers; these are usually good indicators of developments in the curriculum and often include assessments of recent conferences and publications. The volume of published material remorselessly increases and, hence, it is impossible to specify in this short bibliography more than a few British publications, whilst omitting the many relevant publications from the rest of the anglophone world and from non-English speaking sources.

Curriculum — General and Interdisciplinary

Downey, M and Kelly, A (1978) *Moral Education*, Harper and Row
Golby, M *et al* (Eds) (1975) *Curriculum Design*, Open University
HMI (1977–79) *Curriculum 11–16*, Department of Education and Science
HMI ('Matters for Discussion' series) (1978) *Gifted Children in Middle and Secondary Comprehensive Schools*, HMSO
Jenkins, D (Ed) (1976) *Curriculum Studies* (series of six small books), Open Books

Kelly, A V (1977) *The Curriculum*, Harper and Row
Lawton, D *et al* (1978) *Theory and Practice of Curriculum Studies*, Routledge and Kegan Paul.
Richards, C (1984) *The Curriculum: An Introductory Annotated Bibliography*, Nafferton
Sim Kin, D. and J. (Eds) (1984) *Curriculum Development in Education*, Tressell
Taylor, P and Richards, C (1979) *An Introduction to Curriculum Studies*, NFER
Williams, M. (1984) *Designing and Teaching Integrated Courses*, Geographical Association.

Middle Years

Blyth, W and Derricott, R (1977) *The Social Significance of Middle Schools*, Batsford
Gannon, T and Whalley, A (1975) *Middle Schools*, Heinemann
Hargreaves, A and Ticknell, L (Eds) (1980) *Middle Schools: Ideologies, Origins and Practice*, Harper and Row
Owen, R (Ed) (1977) *Middle Years at School*, BBC
Raggett, M and Clarkson, M (Eds) (1974) *The Middle Years Curriculum*, Ward Lock
Schools Council (1972) *Education in the Middle Years*, Working Paper No 42, Evans/Methuen
Schools Council (1975) *Curriculum in the Middle Years*, Working Paper No 55, Evans/Methuen
Schools Council (1977) *Talking, Learning and Writing 8–13*, Evans/Methuen

Humanities and Social Sciences — General

Adams, A (1979) *The Humanities Jungle*, Ward Lock
Blyth, A *et al* Schools Council Place, Time and Society Project, especially (a) *Curriculum planning in history, geography and social science*; (b) *Themes in outline*; (c) *Teaching for concepts*; and (d) *Games and simulations in the classroom*
Hanson, J (Ed) (1981) *The Child at 13: Expectations in the Field of Humanities*, Oxfordshire County Council Education Department
Lawton, D *et al* (1971) *Social Studies 8–13* (Schools Council), Evans/Methuen
Lawton, D and Dufour, B (1973) *The New Social Studies*, Heinemann
Schools Council (1972) *With Objectives in Mind* (Science 5–13), Macdonald

Straddling, R *et al.* (1984) *Teaching Contraversial Issues*, Ed. Arnold
Taylor, J and Walford, R (1978) *Learning and the Simulation Game*,
    Open University Press
Warwick, D (Ed) (1973) *Integrated Studies in Secondary Schools*,
    ULP

Geography

Bailey, P (1974) *Teaching Geography*, David and Charles
Boardman D (1985) — *New Directions in Geographical Education*,
    Falmer Press
Boden, P (1976) *Developments in Geography Teaching*, Open Books
Fien J, *et al* (1985) — *The Geography Teachers' Guide to the
    Classroom*, Macmillan
Graves, N (1972) *New Movements in the Study and Teaching of
    Geography*, Temple Smith
Graves, N (1979) *Curriculum Planning in Geography*, Heinemann
Hall, D (1976) *Geography and the Geography Teacher*, Allen and
    Unwin
HMI/DES (1978) *Teaching of Ideas in Geography*, HMSO
Huckle, J (1983) *Geographical Education: Reflection and Action*,
    OUP
Long, M (Ed) (1975) *Handbook for Geography Teachers*, Methuen
Slater, F (1982) *Learning through Geography*, Heinemann
Tolley H (1984) — *Teaching Geography*, Macmillan
Walford, R (1969) *Games in Geography*, Longman
Walford, R (Ed) (1981) *Signposts for Geography Teaching*, Longman
Williams, M (Ed) (1976) *Geography and the Integrated Curriculum*,
    Heinemann
Classroom Geographer (Journal), Department of Humanities, Bright-
    on Polytechnic

Publications of the Geographical Association

Handbooks on Geography in Secondary, Primary and Middle Schools
Geography (four issues per year)
Teaching Geography (four issues per year)
Teaching Geography Occasional Papers — a series dealing with
    techniques and resources
G Corney (Ed) (1985) — *Geography, Schools and Industry*
G Corney and E Rawlings (Eds.) (1985) — *Teaching Slow Learners
    Through Geography*
A Kent (Ed.) (1985) — *Perspectives on Changing Geography*

R King (Ed.) (1984) — *Geographical Futures*
R Walford (1985) — *Geographical Education for a Multicultural Society*

History

Birt, D and Nichol, J (1975) *Games and Simulations in History,* Longman
Burston, M and Green, C (1972) *Handbook for History Teachers,* Methuen
Chaffer, J and Taylor, L (1972) *History and the History Teacher,* Methuen
DES (1985) — *History in the Primary and Secondary Years,* HMSO
Dickinson A, et al (1985) — *Learning History,* Heinemann
Dickson, A and Lee, P (1978) *History Teaching and Historical Understanding,* Heinemann
Dunning, R (1973) *Local Sources for the Young Historian,* Muller
Fines, J (Ed) (1983) *Teaching History,* Holmes McDougall
Garvey, B and Krug, M (1977) *Models of History Teaching in the Secondary School,* OUP
Godsden, P and Sylvester, D (1968) *History for the Average Child,* Blackwell
Gunning, D (1978) *The Teaching of History,* Croom Helm
ILEA (1982) *Departmental Handbook — History, Learning Materials Service*
Partington, G (1980) *Idea of an Historical Education,* NFER
Richardson, J (1974) *The Local Historian's Encyclopaedia,* Historical Publications
Steel, D and Taylor, L (1973) *Family History in Schools,* Phillimore
Thompson P (1978) — *Voice of the Past,* Oxford U.P.

Publications of the Historical Association

Teaching History (three issues per year)
Occasional publications, especially *Teaching History* series, for example (a) *Studying urban history in schools;* (b) *Resources for teaching of history in secondary schools;* (c) *The new history: theory into practice;* (d) *History and the slow learning child*

Social Sciences

Corlett J and Parry G (1984) — *Anthropology and the Teacher,* ATSS
Crick, B and Porter, A (1978) *Political Education and Political Literacy,* Longman

Economics Association (1978) — *Economics 14–16*, NFER
Gleeson, D and Whitty, G (1976) *Developments in Social Studies Teaching*, Open Books
Gomm, R and McNeill, P (Eds) (1982) *Handbook for Sociology Teachers*, Heinemann
ILEA (1983) *Departmental Handbook: Social Sciences*, Learning Materials Service
Jones B (Ed.) — *Political Issues in Britain Today*, Manchester U.P.
Lee, N (Ed) (1975) *Teaching Economics*, Heinemann
Mathias, P (1973) *Teachers Handbook for Social Studies*, Blandford
Michaelis, J and Keach, E (Eds) (1972) *Teaching Strategies for Elementary School Social Studies*, Peacock
Whitehead, D (Ed) (1974) *Curriculum Development in Economics*, Heinemann
Whitehead, D (Ed) (1979) *Handbook for Economics Teachers*, Heinemann
Various authors — 'Political Realities' Series (Longman)

Association for Teaching of Social Sciences

Social Science Teacher (six issues per year — concerned with education in all the social sciences)
A particularly useful magazine is the popular *New Society*, which provides a regular 'Society to-day' supplement for students.
Modern Studies Association — especially the *Yearbook* (summary of events and issues) and *Modern Studies Journal*

Economics Association

Numerous publications

Politics Association

Numerous publications, including *Teaching Politics*

Environmental Studies

Berry, P (1975) *Sourcebook for Environmental Studies*, Philip
Boon, G *'Townlook'*, *'Rocks in towns'*, etc
Lines, C and Bolwell, L (1971) *Teaching Environmental Studies*, Ginn
Martin, G and Turner, E (Eds) (1972) *Environmental Studies*, Blond

Perry, G *et al* (1976) *Teachers Handbook for Environmental Studies*, Blandford

Schools Council (1972) *Environmental Studies Project Teachers Guide: Case studies, Starting from rocks, Starting from maps*, Hart Davis

Schools Council (1974) *Project Environment*: (a) *Education for the environment*; (b) *Learning from trails*, Longman

Schools Council (1976) *Out and About*, Evans/Methuen

The Town and Country Planning Association publishes the *Bulletin of Environmental Education* every month.

Other information is in the *Directory of Environmental Literature and Teaching Aids* from the Council for Environmental Education.

Urban and Rural Studies

Briggs, K (1971) *Fieldwork in Urban Geography*, Oliver and Boyd

Bull, G (1971) *Town Study Companion*, Hulton

Clout, H (1972) *Rural Geography*, Pergamon

Cross, M and Daniel, P (1969) *Fieldwork for Geography Classes*, McGraw Hill

Driscoll, K (1976) *Town Study*, Philip

Ward, A and Fyson, C (1973) *Streetwork*, Routledge

Assessment and Evaluation

Cooper, K (1976) *Evaluation, Assessment and Record Keeping in History, Geography and Social Science*, Collins for the Schools Council

Deale, R (1975) *Assessment and Testing in the Secondary School*, Evans/Methuen for the Schools Council

Hudson, B (Eds) (1973) *Assessment Techniques*, Methuen

Macintosh, H (1976a) *Assessing Attainment in the Classroom*, Hodder and Stoughton

Macintosh, H (1976b) *Assessment and the Secondary School Teacher*, Routledge

Scottish Education Department (1979) *Issues in Educational Assessment*, HMSO

Wiseman, S and Pidgeon, D (1972) *Curriculum Evaluation*, NFER

Assessment of Performance Unit

Publications from the Department of Education and Science, Elizabeth House, York Road, London, SE1 7PH

Particularly useful publications *Language Performance and Assessment: Why, What and How?*
The most useful assessment material, of a conventional type, for pupils use that I have discovered are the Study Skills sections of the Bristol Achievement Tests and of the Richmond Tests (both published by Nelson). 'Study Skills' is concerned, amongst other matters, with a number of skills associated with geography, such as map interpretation, but there is little of relevance to history and the social sciences. More work needs to be done on supplementing and extending this published material.

Resources, Study Skills and Computers

Adams, A and Jones, E (1983) *Teaching Humanities in the Microelectronic Age*, Open University
Alexander, E (1974) *Museums and How to Use Them*, Batsford
Beswick, N (1977) *Resource Based Learning*, Heinemann
Burnett, J (1979) *Successful Study* ('Teach Yourself Books'), Hodder
Buzan, T (1983) — *Use your Head*, BBC
Fairley, J (1977) *History Teaching through Museums*, Longmans
Fergus, A (1977) *Finding Out from Books* (Pupils' Book), Hulton
Forester, T (Ed) 1983 — *The Microelectronics Revolution*, Blackwell
Herring, J (1978) *Teaching Library Skills in Schools*, NFER
Horne, D (1984) — *Great Museum*, Pluto
Irving, A (1985) — *Study and Information Skills Across the Curriculum*, Heinemann
Kent, A (Ed) (1983) *Geography Teaching and the Micro*, Longman
Mckeown, S (1983) — *Effective Learning Skills*, ILEA
Payne, A *et al* (1980) *Computer Software for Schools*, Pitman
Rowntree, D (1976) *Learn How to Study*, Macdonald and Janes
Schools Council (1972) *Pterodactyls and Old Lace*, Evans/Methuen
Shephard, I D *et al* (1980) *Computer Assisted Learning in Geography*, Geographical Association
Sieghart, P (Ed) 1982 — *Microchips with Everything*, Comedia

Fiction

Particularly useful publications from:

1 *National Book League*
   (a) *Stories and Settings* series, for example *The Americans, Europe and USSR, Africa*
   (b) Other lists such as *Fiction 9–13*
2 *Library Association* — Youth Libraries Group

(a)   *Storylines* series, for example, *Romans to Vikings, Into Space, World War Two, Prehistory*
3   *Schools Library Association:* short annotated bibliographies, such as *Fiction, Verse and Legend* and *The World in Stories*.

Classics

Cook, E (1969) *The Ordinary and The Fabulous*, CUP
HMI/DES ('Matters for Discussion' series) (1977) *Classics in Comprehensive Schools*, HMSO
Sharwood Smith, J (1977) *On Teaching Classics*, Routledge

Racism and Prejudice

Beddoe, D (1983) — *Discovering Women's History*, Pandora
Husband, C (Ed) (1982) *'Race' in Britain*, Hutchinson
Humana, C (1983) — *World Human Rights Guide*, Hutchinson
McDiarmid, G and Pratt, D (1971) *Teaching Prejudice*, Ontario Institute for Studies in Education, Toronto
Milner, D (1983) *Children and Race*, Penguin
Minority Rights Group (1984) *Teaching about Prejudice*
New Internationalist (1985) — *Women: A World Report*, Methuen
Pilkington, A (1984) — *Race Relations in Britain*, U.T.P.
Rowbottom, S (1977) — *Hidden from History*
Whyld, J (Ed) (1983) — *Sexism and the Secondary Curriculum*, Harper and Row
Women and Geography Study Group (1984) — *Geography and Gender*, Hutchinson
Zimet, S (1977) *Print and Prejudice*, Hodder

World Studies

Bale, J (Ed) (1983) *Third World: issues and approaches*, Geographical Association
Bradford, W (1985) — *Development*, ATSS
Council for World Development Education (1985) *Development Puzzle*
Heard, A (1985) — *Teachers' Guide to Development Education* Welsh Centre for International Affairs
Hicks, D (1981) *Minorities*, Heinemann
Hicks, D and Townley, C (1982) *Teaching World Studies*, Longman
Morris, M (1983) *Development in the Third World*, Oxford

Mountjoy, A (Ed) *Third World: problems and perspectives*, Macmillan
World Studies Project at the University of York publishes the very useful quarterly *World Studies Journal* as well as Key Texts such as *Learning for Change in World Society* and *Ideas into Action*.
There are a considerable number of journals which deal with race relations in Britain in a general world context that have articles on the school curriculum which vary in quality and value. Amongst the more valuable are *New Community, New Internationalist* and *New Era*.
There is a useful compendium of educational materials from the Community Relations Commission. It is called *Education for a Multiracial Society*.
Recent publications from the Geography Department of the University of London Institute of Education are concerned with the relationships between the teaching of geography and social inequalities within a national and global context. The conference report *Racist Society; Geography Curriculum* is an example.

Media and Language in Humanities

D'Arcy, P (1973) *Reading for Meaning*, Vol 2, Hutchinson
HMSO (1975) *A Language for Life* (Bullock Report), HMSO
Marland, M (1977) *Language Across the Curriculum*, Heinemann
Masterman, L (1978) *Teaching About Television*, Macmillan
Masterman, L (1986) *Teaching the Media*, Comedia
Neelands, J (1985) *Making Sense of Drama*, Heinemann
O'Neill, C and Lambert, A. (1982) *Drama Structures*, Hutchinson
Torbe, M (1981) *Language, Teaching and Learning Series*, Ward Lock
The Schools Council Project 'Writing across the Curriculum 1976' — publications include 'Language and Learning in Humanities'. (The Project's work has been heavily criticized, but the viewpoints expressed by the Project Team are worth examination.)

Mixed Ability

There are many publications, but three of the better 'handbooks' are:
Kelly, A V (Ed) (1975) *Case Studies in Mixed Ability Teaching*, Harper and Row
Kelly, A V (1977) *Teaching Mixed Ability Classes*, Harper and Row
Wragg, E C (Ed) (1976) *Teaching Mixed Ability Groups*, David and Charles